Las trampas del inglés

Ron Murphy – M.ª José Rodellar

LAS TRAMPAS DEL INGLÉS

dve
PUBLISHING

© Editorial De Vecchi, S. A. 2019
© [2019] Confidential Concepts International Ltd., Ireland
Subsidiary company of Confidential Concepts Inc, USA
ISBN: 978-1-64461-905-6

Índice

SOLUCIONARIO

Introducción

Muchos de nosotros traduciríamos sin ningún problema la frase «*He is a very candid person*» como «es una persona muy cándida». Pero, ¡cuidado!, sin apenas sospecharlo habríamos caído en una de las múltiples y engañosas trampas del inglés, porque *candid* no significa «cándido» sino «franco», de manera que la traducción correcta sería: «es una persona muy franca».

Las diferencias léxicas entre el inglés y el español provocan frecuentes confusiones entre hispanohablantes: traducciones literales e incorrectas, términos ingleses que tienen correspondencias múltiples en español, preposiciones que cambian el significado de los verbos. Todas estas particularidades léxicas de la lengua inglesa son «trampas» en las que, como en el ejemplo anterior, fácil e inconscientemente podemos caer. El objetivo de este manual es precisamente sacar a la luz todas estas «trampas». Para ello hemos recopilado los términos, giros y expresiones que suelen provocar confusión, hemos anotado su significado correcto, los hemos clasificado y, finalmente, hemos presentado la palabra que debe utilizarse para expresar el significado erróneo. Por ejemplo: *actual* significa «real» (significado correcto) y no «actual» (significado erróneo), como parece; en cambio, en inglés, para expresar «actual» (significado diferente) se emplea *present* (palabra que expresa el significado erróneo).

Este es, pues, un manual de inglés destinado a ampliar y afianzar el vocabulario, a aprender a expresarse correctamente y a conocer y practicar los temidos *phrasal verbs* (verbos seguidos de preposición), su aplicación y traducción a la lengua española. Entenendemos que una larga lista de términos y giros podría resultar una buena obra de consulta, pero nuestra intención va más lejos. Los usos de una lengua sólo se aprenden con la práctica continuada, por ello, además de las diferentes clasificaciones de términos en español e inglés que encontrará en el libro, le ofrecemos una amplia batería de ejercicios, con su solucionario al final del libro, para que pueda comprobar sus progresos.

Términos engañosos

C omo hemos comentado en la introducción de la obra, algunos términos ingleses se parecen mucho a otros españoles. Sin embargo, no siempre esta semejanza aparente corresponde a una semejanza semántica.

Dicho de otro modo, las palabras se parecen pero sus significados no, por lo que nos encontramos ante palabras «engañosas» que pueden inducirnos a usarlas erróneamente.

A continuación, mostramos una serie palabras inglesas agrupadas en dos listas según la mayor o menor semejanza con su correspondiente española:

• Términos de significado distinto: la palabra inglesa y la palabra española sólo se parecen en la forma, pero el significado de una no tiene nada que ver con el de la otra. Se trata de los términos más engañosos. Junto al significado erróneo aparece la palabra inglesa (entre paréntesis y en cursiva) que debe utilizarse para expresar dicho significado.

• Términos con acepciones comunes pero usados habitualmente en otro sentido: en este caso, la palabra inglesa tiene el mismo significado que su semejante española, pero este es sólo uno de sus varios significados y no precisamente el más utilizado.

Términos de significado distinto

ABANDON
— *Significa*: abandonar para siempre
— *No significa*: abandonar, marcharse *(to leave)*

ACCEPTATION
— *Significa*: acepción
— *No significa*: aceptación *(acceptance)*

ACCORD
— *Significa*: otorgar, concordar
— *No significa*: acordar *(to agree upon)*

ACCOST
— *Significa*: dirigirse a alguien con fines deshonestos
— *No significa*: acostar, acostarse *(to put to bed, to go to bed)*

ACTUAL
— *Significa*: real
— *No significa*: actual *(present)*

ACTUALLY
— *Significa*: realmente
— *No significa*: actualmente *(at present)*

ADEPT
— *Significa*: experto
— *No significa*: adepto *(follower)*

ADHERENT
— *Significa*: partidario
— *No significa*: adherente *(adhesive)*

ADJUDICATE
— *Significa*: dictaminar
— *No significa*: adjudicar *(to award)*

ADVERT
— *Significa*: referirse
— *No significa*: advertir *(to warn)*

ADVISE
— *Significa*: aconsejar, notificar
— *No significa*: avisar *(to warn)*

AFFRONT
— *Significa*: ofender
— *No significa*: afrontar *(to face)*

AGENDA
— *Significa*: orden del día
— *No significa*: agenda *(appointment book)*

ALIENATED
— *Significa*: apartado; esquivado; despreciado; confiscado; transferido
— *No significa*: alienado (loco) *(insane, crazy)*

ALTERNATE
— *Significa*: alternar, turnar
— *No significa*: alternar con gente *(to mix with, to be sociable)*

ANIMADVERSION
— *Significa*: crítica severa
— *No significa*: animadversión (ojeriza) *(ill-will)*

ANNOUNCE
— *Significa*: anunciar, dar una noticia
— *No significa*: anunciar (hacer publicidad) *(to advertise)*

APERTURE
— *Significa*: abertura, rendija, resquicio
— *No significa*: apertura *(inauguration, opening)*

APPARATUS
— *Significa*: aparato mecánico o fisiológico
— *No significa*: aparato *(set, instrument, device)*

APRECIATE
— *Significa*: agradecer; valorar, subir de valor
— *No significa*: apreciar (tener cariño; percibir) *(to like, to love, to be fond of)*

APROBE
— *Significa*: aprobar (estar conforme)
— *No significa*: aprobar un examen *(to pass)*

ARGUMENT
— *Significa*: discusión, razonamiento
— *No significa*: argumento de una obra *(plot)*

ARTIFICE
— *Significa*: artificio, habilidad
— *No significa*: artífice *(author)*

ARTIST
— *Significa*: artista de bellas artes
— *No significa*: artista dramático *(actor/actress)*

ASPIRATE
— *Significa*: aspirar (fonética); succionar
— *No significa*: aspirar (inspirar; tener aspiraciones) *(to breathe in, to aspire)*

ASPIRE
— *Significa*: aspirar, ambicionar
— *No significa*: aspirar (inspirar; succionar) *(to breathe in; to aspirate)*

ASSIST
— *Significa*: asistir (ayudar)
— *No significa*: asistir (estar presente, acudir) *(to attend)*

ASSISTANCE
— *Significa*: asistencia (ayuda)
— *No significa*: asistencia (presencia, comparecencia) *(attendance)*

ASSISTANT
— *Significa*: asistente (ayudante)
— *No significa*: asistente militar; asistenta *(orderly; cleaning lady)*

ATTIC
— *Significa*: buhardilla
— *No significa*: ático *(top floor)*

BACCALAUREATE
— *Significa*: licenciatura universitaria
— *No significa*: bachillerato *(high school)*

BACHELOR
— *Significa*: licenciado; soltero
— *No significa*: bachiller *(high school graduate)*

BARRACKS
— *Significa*: cuartel
— *No significa*: barracas *(huts)*

BILLION
— *Significa*: mil millones
— *No significa*: billón (*a million millions, a trillion*)

CABIN
— *Significa*: camarote; cabaña, cabina de avión
— *No significa*: cabina telefónica (*booth*)

CAMP
— *Significa*: campamento
— *No significa*: campo (*field, country*)

CANDID
— *Significa*: franco, sincero
— *No significa*: cándido (*ingenuous*)

CARBON
— *Significa*: carbono
— *No significa*: carbón (*coal*)

CARPET
— *Significa*: moqueta, alfombra
— *No significa*: carpeta (*folder*)

CARTON
— *Significa*: caja de cartón
— *No significa*: cartón (*cardboard*)

CARTOON
— *Significa*: dibujos animados
— *No significa*: cartón (*cardboard*)

CASTOR
— *Significa*: rueda de debajo de un mueble; frasco
— *No significa*: castor *(beaver)*

CASUALTY
— *Significa*: baja, víctima, muerto
— *No significa*: casualidad *(chance, coincidence)*

CHARLATAN
— *Significa*: charlatán (embaucador; curandero)
— *No significa*: charlatán (hablador) *(talkative)*

COLLAR
— *Significa*: cuello de camisa; collar de animal
— *No significa*: collar (joya) *(necklace)*

COLLEGE
— *Significa*: universidad
— *No significa*: colegio *(school)*

COMMODITY
— *Significa*: mercancía; productos básicos
— *No significa*: comodidad *(comfort)*

COMPLACENT
— *Significa*: satisfecho consigo mismo
— *No significa*: complaciente *(complaisant)*

COMPLEXION
— *Significa*: color del cutis
— No significa: complexión *(physical constitution)*

COMPLIMENT
— *Significa*: cumplido
— *No significa*: complemento, accesorio
(complement)

COMPOSITOR
— *Significa*: cajista de imprenta
— *No significa*: compositor musical *(composer)*

COMPREHENSIVE
— *Significa*: completo, que lo incluye todo
— *No significa*: comprensivo *(understanding)*

COMPROMISE
— *Significa*: compromiso (acuerdo)
— *No significa*: compromiso (obligación; situación
  difícil) *(obligation, engagement; predicament)*

CONCOURSE
— *Significa*: concurso (concurrencia)
— *No significa*: concurso (competición) *(contest)*

CONDUCTOR
— *Significa*: cobrador, revisor; director de orquesta,
  coro
— *No significa*: conductor de vehículos *(driver)*

CONFECTIONER
— *Significa*: pastelero
— *No significa*: confeccionador *(maker)*

CONFERENCE
— *Significa*: congreso
— *No significa*: conferencia (disertación; llamada a larga distancia) *(lecture; long distance call)*

CONFIDENT
— *Significa*: seguro
— *No significa*: confidente *(confidant; spy)*

CONJURATION
— *Significa*: conjuro
— *No significa*: conjuración *(plot, conspiracy)*

CONJURE
— *Significa*: invocar; hacer juegos de manos; hacer aparecer
— *No significa*: conjurarse *(to plot; to conspire)*

CONJURER/CONJUROR
— *Significa*: prestidigitador
— *No significa*: conjurar *(plotter, conspirator)*

CONSEQUENT
— *Significa*: consecuente (derivado de consecuencia, lógico)
— *No significa*: consecuente (persona) *(consistent)*

CONSPICUOUS
— *Significa*: visible, llamativo
— *No significa*: conspicuo (notable) *(outstanding)*

CONSTIPATED
— *Significa*: estreñido
— *No significa*: constipado *(to have a cold)*

CONTENT
— *Significa*: satisfecho
— *No significa*: contento (feliz) *(happy, gay, joyful)*

CONVENIENT
— *Significa*: cómodo; a mano; oportuno
— *No significa*: conveniente (beneficioso, aconsejable, apropiado) *(advisable, suitable)*

CREATURE
— *Significa*: criatura (ser viviente)
— *No significa*: criatura (niño pequeño) *(baby, young child)*

CRIME
— *Significa*: delito
— *No significa*: crimen (delito de sangre o muy grave) *(murder; felony)*

CUP
— *Significa*: taza
— *No significa*: copa *(glass; drink)*

CURRENT
— *Significa*: actual
— *No significa*: corriente *(ordinary; running [water])*

CYNIC
— *Significa*: escéptico
— *No significa*: cínico *(barefaced, bold)*

DECEPTION
— *Significa*: engaño
— *No significa*: decepción *(disappointment)*

DEMAND
— *Significa*: exigir, reclamar
— *No significa*: demandar (judicialmente) *(to sue)*

DEPENDENT
— *Significa*: dependiente (el que depende de otro)
— *No significa*: dependiente de comercio *(sales clerk, shop assistant)*

DIRECTIONS
— *Significa*: instrucciones
— *No significa*: direcciones *(addresses)*

DISGRACE
— *Significa*: deshonra
— *No significa*: desgracia *(misfortune)*

DISGUST
— *Significa*: repugnancia
— *No significa*: disgusto, desazón *(irritation; quarrel; sorrow)*

DISPOSE OF
— *Significa*: deshacerse de
— *No significa*: disponer de *(to have)*

DORMITORY
— *Significa*: dormitorio colectivo
— *No significa*: dormitorio particular *(bedroom)*

EDIFICATION
— *Significa*: formación moral
— *No significa*: edificio *(building)*

EDIT
— *Significa*: corregir y preparar textos para publi-
carlos
— *No significa*: editar *(to publish)*

EDITOR
— *Significa*: redactor
— *No significa*: editor *(publisher)*

EDITORIAL
— *Significa*: editorial (artículo de fondo)
— *No significa*: empresa editorial *(publishing firm or
company)*

EDUCATED
— *Significa*: culto
— *No significa*: educado, cortés *(well-mannered,
polite)*

EDUCATION
— *Significa*: cultura
— *No significa*: buena educación, buenos modales *(good manners)*

EFFECTIVELY
— *Significa*: en la práctica
— *No significa*: efectivamente *(in fact)*

ELEMENTAL
— *Significa*: de los elementos
— *No significa*: elemental, básico, fundamental *(elementary, basic)*

EMBARRASSED
— *Significa*: turbado, avergonzado
— *No significa*: embarazada *(pregnant)*

ENTERTAIN
— *Significa*: recibir invitados
— *No significa*: entretener (retener); entretenerse (retrasarse) *(to keep, to loiter)*

ERR
— *Significa*: errar (equivocarse)
— *No significa*: errar (vagar) *(to wander)*

ESTIMATE
— *Significa*: estimar (calcular)
— *No significa*: estimar (apreciar) *(to esteem)*

EVENTUAL
— *Significa*: que llega con el tiempo
— *No significa*: eventual, provisional *(temporary)*

EVENTUALLY
— *Significa*: con el tiempo
— *No significa*: eventualmente *(provisionally, temporarily)*

EXIGENCE
— *Significa*: necesidad urgente
— *No significa*: exigencia *(demand)*

EXIT
— *Significa*: salida
— *No significa*: éxito *(success)*

EXPECTATION
— *Significa*: expectativa
— *No significa*: expectación *(expectancy)*

EXPEDIENT
— *Significa*: estratagema; ventajoso
— *No significa*: expediente *(record)*

EXPERIMENT
— *Significa*: experimentar (hacer experimentos, probar, ensayar)
— *No significa*: experimentar (sentir, notar) *(to experience)*

EXPLODE
— *Significa*: explotar (estallar)
— *No significa*: explotar (sacar provecho)
  (to exploit)

EXPOSITION
— *Significa*: presentación oral o escrita
— *No significa*: exposición artística *(exhibition)*

EXTENDED
— *Significa*: extendido, prolongado
— *No significa*: extendido (generalizado; disperso)
  (widespread; spread out)

EXTENUATE
— *Significa*: atenuar
— *No significa*: extenuar *(to weaken)*

EXTENUATED
— *Significa*: atenuado
— *No significa*: extenuado (rendido, fatigado)
  (exhausted)

FABRIC
— *Significa*: tejido
— *No significa*: fábrica *(factory)*

FACTION
— *Significa*: facción (banda rebelde)
— *No significa*: facción (del rostro) *(feature)*

FAMILIAR
— *Significa*: familiar (adjetivo)
— *No significa*: familiar (sustantivo), pariente *(relative)*

FASTIDIOUS
— *Significa*: quisquilloso, exigente
— *No significa*: fastidioso *(troublesome, tedious)*

FEAST
— *Significa*: banquete; fiesta religiosa
— *No significa*: fiesta (reunión social; día no laborable) *(party, holiday)*

FIRM
— *Significa*: firma (empresa)
— *No significa*: firma (signatura) *(signature)*

FLORID
— *Significa*: sonrosado; florido (recargado)
— *No significa*: florido (con flores) *(flowery; in bloom)*

FORMAL
— *Significa*: ceremonioso; de etiqueta
— *No significa*: formal (serio) *(reliable, upright)*

GABERDINE
— *Significa*: tejido de gabardina
— *No significa*: gabardina (prenda) *(raincoat)*

GUARD
— *Significa*: guardar (proteger)
— *No significa*: guardar (conservar) *(to keep, to save)*

GENIAL
— *Significa*: afable
— *No significa*: genial *(ingenious)*

GENIALITY
— *Significa*: afabilidad
— *No significa*: genialidad *(stroke of genius)*

GENIUS
— *Significa*: genio (persona de talento)
— *No significa*: genio (carácter) *(temper)*

GENTLY
— *Significa*: con suavidad
— *No significa*: gentilmente *(kindly)*

GRACIOUS
— *Significa*: gracioso (garboso; gentil)
— *No significa*: gracioso (chistoso) *(funny; witty)*

GRATIFICATION
— *Significa*: satisfacción
— *No significa*: gratificación *(bonus, reward)*

GRATIFY
— *Significa*: dar satisfacción
— *No significa*: gratificar (recompensar) *(to reward)*

GRENADE
— *Significa*: granada (proyectil)
— *No significa*: granada (fruto) *(pomegranate)*

HUMANE
— *Significa*: humano (bondadoso)
— *No significa*: humano (del hombre) *(human)*

IDIOM
— *Significa*: modismo
— *No significa*: idioma *(language)*

IGNORE
— *Significa*: hacer caso omiso
— *No significa*: ignorar (desconocer) *(not to know)*

ILLUSTRATED
— *Significa*: ilustrado (con ilustraciones)
— *No significa*: ilustrado (instruido) *(learned)*

IMPORTUNE
— *Significa*: insistir en una petición
— *No significa*: importunar *(to bother)*

IMPREGNABLE
— *Significa*: inexpugnable
— *No significa*: impregnable *(saturable)*

IMPROVABLE
— *Significa*: mejorable
— *No significa*: improbable *(unlikely)*

INADEQUATE
— *Significa*: insuficiente
— *No significa*: inadecuado *(inappropriate)*

INCONVENIENT
— *Significa*: molesto, incómodo
— *No significa*: inconveniente (sustantivo)
   (objection)

INCORPORATE
— *Significa*: incorporar, unir, unirse
— *No significa*: incorporarse (erguirse) *(to sit up; to straighten)*

INDIGNANT
— *Significa*: indignado
— *No significa*: indignante *(infuriating, outrageous)*

INDISCRETE
— *Significa*: homogéneo
— *No significa*: indiscreto *(indiscreet)*

INFIDEL
— *Significa*: pagano
— *No significa*: infiel (desleal) *(disloyal)*

INFORMAL
— *Significa*: informal (sin protocolo)
— *No significa*: informal (indigno de confianza) *(unreliable)*

INGENUITY
— *Significa*: ingenio
— *No significa*: ingenuidad *(ingenuousness)*

INHABITABLE
— *Significa*: habitable
— *No significa*: inhabitable *(uninhabitable)*

INSPIRE
— *Significa*: inspirar (infundir ideas)
— *No significa*: inspirar (aspirar) *(to breathe in)*

INTEND
— *Significa*: tener intención
— *No significa*: intentar *(to try)*

INTIMATE
— *Significa*: sugerir,insinuar
— *No significa*: intimar *(to become intimate)*

INVERT
— *Significa*: invertir (alterar la posición)
— *No significa*: invertir (emplear dinero) *(to invest)*

INVIDIOUS
— *Significa*: irritante, odioso
— *No significa*: envidioso *(envious)*

LAGOON
— *Significa*: albufera
— *No significa*: laguna *(small lake)*

LECTURE
— *Significa*: conferencia
— *No significa*: lectura *(reading)*

LIBRARY
— *Significa*: biblioteca
— *No significa*: librería *(bookstore)*

LOCAL
— *Significa*: lugareño; local (adjetivo)
— *No significa*: local (espacio cerrado) *(premises, buildings)*

MALIGN
— *Significa*: difamar; calumniar
— *No significa*: maligno *(malignant)*

MARMALADE
— *Significa*: mermelada de naranja amarga o de otros cítricos
— *No significa*: mermelada en general *(jam)*

MEASURE
— *Significa*: medida
— *No significa*: mesura *(moderation)*

MISERABLE
— *Significa*: miserable (pobre); desgraciado
— *No significa*: miserable (canalla) *(wicked, mean person)*

MORAL
— *Significa*: moraleja; moral (adj.)
— *No significa*: moral (estado anímico; principios)
  (morale)

MOTORIST
— *Significa*: automovilista
— *No significa*: motorista *(motorcyclist)*

MYSTIFY
— *Significa*: dejar perplejo
— *No significa*: mistificar *(to hoax)*

NOTE
— *Significa*: nota musical; apunte; observar
— *No significa*: nota (calificación); notar (percibir)
  (grade; feel, realize)

NOTICE
— *Significa*: aviso, anuncio
— *No significa*: noticia *(news)*

NOVEL
— *Significa*: original, nuevo; novela
— *No significa*: novel *(beginner)*

OBSEQUIOUS
— *Significa*: servil
— *No significa*: obsequioso *(obliging)*

OCCURRENCE
— *Significa*: suceso
— *No significa*: ocurrencia (idea ingeniosa) *(witty idea)*

OCCURRENT
— *Significa*: que ocurre
— *No significa*: ocurrente (ingenioso, agudo, gracioso) *(witty)*

OFFICIAL
— *Significa*: funcionario oficial (adj.)
— *No significa*: oficial (militar) *(officer)*

OFFICIOUS
— *Significa*: entrometido
— *No significa*: oficioso *(unofficial)*

ORDINARY
— *Significa*: ordinario (corriente)
— *No significa*: ordinario (vulgar) *(vulgar)*

PARENT
— *Significa*: padre o madre
— *No significa*: pariente *(relative)*

PARENTS
— *Significa*: padres
— *No significa*: parientes *(relatives)*

PARSIMONY
— *Significa*: moderación en los gastos
— *No significa*: parsimonia (lentitud) *(calmness)*

PARTICULAR
— *Significa*: particular (especial concreto)
— *No significa*: particular (privado) *(private)*

PERCEIVE
— *Significa*: percibir (captar)
— *No significa*: percibir (cobrar) *(to receive)*

PERIODICAL
— *Significa*: publicación periódica
— *No significa*: periódico *(newspaper)*

PERMUTE
— *Significa*: cambiar el orden
— *No significa*: permutar *(to exchange)*

PETROL
— *Significa*: gasolina (en británico)
— *No significa*: petróleo *(oil, petroleum)*

PETULANCE
— *Significa*: susceptibilidad, irritabilidad
— *No significa*: petulancia (engreimiento) *(arrogance)*

PETULANT
— *Significa*: impaciente, irritable
— *No significa*: petulante (engreído) *(conceited)*

PHYSICIAN
— *Significa*: médico
— *No significa*: físico (*physicist*)

POLICY
— *Significa*: norma, principio; póliza
— *No significa*: política de gobierno (*politics*)

POLITIC
— *Significa*: sagaz, prudente
— *No significa*: político (dedicado o relativo a la política; que tiene parentesco por afinidad) (*political; in law*)

PORTER
— *Significa*: mozo de estación
— *No significa*: portero (*doorman; goalkeeper*)

PRACTITIONER
— *Significa*: médico
— *No significa*: practicante (*practicing [adj.]; medical assistant, nurse*)

PRECINCT
— *Significa*: recinto
— *No significa*: precinto (*seal*)

PRECIOUS
— *Significa*: precioso (valioso)
— *No significa*: precioso (bonito) (*beautiful*)

PRECISE
— *Significa*: preciso (exacto)
— *No significa*: preciso (necesario) *(necessary)*

PREOCCUPIED
— *Significa*: absorto, distraído; ocupado
— *No significa*: preocupado *(worried)*

PREVENT
— *Significa*: impedir
— *No significa*: prevenir *(to warn; to take precautions)*

PROFESSOR
— *Significa*: profesor universitario
— *No significa*: profesor (de cualquier otro nivel académico) *(teacher)*

PROFOUND
— *Significa*: profundo (de pensamiento)
— *No significa*: profundo (en el espacio) *(deep)*

PROSPECT
— *Significa*: perspectiva
— *No significa*: prospecto *(leaflet)*

PROVE
— *Significa*: probar (demostrar)
— *No significa*: probar (someter a prueba) *(to try; to test; to taste)*

QUALIFICATIONS
— *Significa*: preparación, aptitud
— *No significa*: calificaciones escolares *(grades)*

QUIET
— *Significa*: silencioso
— *No significa*: quieto *(still)*

QUOTA
— *Significa*: cuota (parte proporcional)
— *No significa*: cuota (contribución monetaria) *(fee)*

RARE
— *Significa*: raro (poco frecuente)
— *No significa*: raro (extraño) *(strange)*

RECLAMATION
— *Significa*: recuperación de materiales a partir de desechos
— *No significa*: reclamación *(complaint)*

RECOGNIZE
— *Significa*: reconocer (admitir; identificar)
— *No significa*: reconocer (examinar) *(to examine)*

RECOLLECT
— *Significa*: recordar
— *No significa*: recolectar, recoger la cosecha *(to collect, to harvest)*

RECOLLECTION
— *Significa*: recuerdo
— *No significa*: recolección *(collection, harvest)*

RECORD
— *Significa*: registro, grabar; disco
— *No significa*: recordar *(to remember)*

RECUR
— *Significa*: repetirse
— *No significa*: recurrir a *(to resort to)*

REFRAIN
— *Significa*: estribillo
— *No significa*: refrán *(saying)*

REFUND
— *Significa*: reembolsar; reembolso
— *No significa*: refundir *(recast)*

REGALE
— *Significa*: agasajar
— *No significa*: regalar *(to give [as] a gift)*

REGISTER
— *Significa*: registrar (inscribir); registro; certificar
— *No significa*: registrar (inspeccionar) *(to search)*

REGULAR
— *Significa*: regular (sin variaciones)
— *No significa*: regular (mediano) *(average)*

REIGN
— *Significa*: reinado; reinar
— *No significa*: reino *(kingdom)*

RELATION
— *Significa*: relación; relato; pariente
— *No significa*: relación (lista) *(list)*

RELEVANT
— *Significa*: pertinente, adecuado
— *No significa*: relevante *(outstanding)*

RELIEVE
— *Significa*: aliviar; relevar
— *No significa*: relieve *(relief)*

REMOVE
— *Significa*: retirar
— *No significa*: remover *(to stir up)*

RENT
— *Significa*: renta (lo que paga en dinero un arren-
    datario)
— *No significa*: renta (beneficio que rinde algo)
    (income)

RESIST
— *Significa*: resistirse a una tentación
— *No significa*: resistir (soportar, aguantar) *(to endure,
    to stand)*

RESULT
— *Significa*: resultar (ser consecuencia)
— *No significa*: resultar (ocurrir o ser finalmente) *(to turn out to be)*

RESUME
— *Significa*: reanudar
— *No significa*: resumir *(to summarize)*

REUNION
— *Significa*: reencuentro
— *No significa*: reunión *(meeting)*

REVOLVE
— *Significa*: girar
— *No significa*: revolver *(to stir up)*

ROTUND
— *Significa*: gordo; sonoro
— *No significa*: rotundo (completo; expresivo y preciso) *(complete; categorical)*

RUBRIC
— *Significa*: encabezamiento
— *No significa*: rúbrica *(flourish)*

RUMOUR
— *Significa*: rumor (habladuría)
— *No significa*: rumor (ruido vago o ruido confuso de voces) *(murmur, buzz)*

SALVAGE
— *Significa*: salvamento
— *No significa*: salvaje *(savage)*

SANE
— *Significa*: cuerdo
— *No significa*: sano *(healthy)*

SANITY
— *Significa*: salud mental
— *No significa*: sanidad *(health)*

SCANDAL
— *Significa*: escándalo (hecho inmoral)
— *No significa*: escándalo (alboroto) *(uproar)*

SCANDALOUS
— *Significa*: escandaloso (inmoral); chismoso
— *No significa*: escandaloso (ruidoso) *(noisy)*

SCENARIO
— *Significa*: guión
— *No significa*: escenario *(stage)*

SCHEME
— *Significa*: plan
— *No significa*: esquema *(outline)*

SCHOLAR
— *Significa*: erudito
— *No significa*: escolar *(school)*

SEMBLANCE
— *Significa*: apariencia
— *No significa*: semblanza *(biographical profile)*

SENSIBLE
— *Significa*: sensato; perceptible
— *No significa*: sensible (capaz de sentir física y moralmente) *(sensitive)*

SENTENCE
— *Significa*: oración gramatical; sentencia judicial
— *No significa*: sentencia (máxima) *(maxim)*

SERIOUS
— *Significa*: serio (grave; solemne)
— *No significa*: serio (digno de confianza, real, verdadero) *(reliable)*

SOLICITOUS
— *Significa*: preocupado
— *No significa*: solícito *(kind, diligent)*

SOLICITUDE
— *Significa*: preocupación
— *No significa*: solicitud (diligencia, amabilidad; petición) *(kindness, diligence; application)*

SPADE
— *Significa*: pala; espada (naipe)
— *No significa*: espada (arma) *(sword)*

SPLENDID
— *Significa*: espléndido (magnífico)
— *No significa*: espléndido (generoso) *(generous, open-handed)*

SQUALID
— *Significa*: miserable
— *No significa*: escuálido *(thin, skinny)*

STAMP
— *Significa*: sello
— *No significa*: estampa *(picture, image)*

STRANGER
— *Significa*: extraño
— *No significa*: extranjero *(foreigner)*

STUDIO
— *Significa*: estudio de artista; apartamento de una habitación
— *No significa*: estudio (acción de estudiar; despacho) *(study)*

SUBURB
— *Significa*: zona residencial de las afueras
— *No significa*: barrio pobre de las afueras *(slums)*

SUCCEED
— *Significa*: tener éxito; suceder en un cargo
— *No significa*: suceder (ocurrir) *(to happen)*

SUCCESS
— *Significa*: éxito
— *No significa*: suceso *(event)*

SUFFOCATE
— *Significa*: ahogar, ahogarse
— *No significa*: sofocar (apagar); acalorarse *(to extinguish; to get hot, excited)*

SUPPORT
— *Significa*: soportar (sostener un peso); mantener económicamente
— *No significa*: soportar (aguantar a una persona o situación desagradable) *(to put up with)*

SUSPEND
— *Significa*: suspender (interrumpir; colgar)
— *No significa*: suspender un examen *(to fail)*

SUSPICIOUS
— *Significa*: suspicaz; sospechoso (adj.)
— *No significa*: sospechoso (sust.) *(suspect)*

SYMPATHETIC
— *Significa*: compasivo, comprensivo
— *No significa*: simpático *(friendly, nice)*

SYMPATHIZE
— *Significa*: compadecerse, comprender
— *No significa*: simpatizar *(to like, to get along)*

SYMPATHY
— *Significa*: compasión, comprensión
— *No significa*: simpatía *(affection)*

TOPIC
— *Significa*: tema
— *No significa*: tópico (lugar común) *(commonplace)*

TRADUCE
— *Significa*: calumniar, difamar
— *No significa*: traducir *(to translate)*

TRADUCER
— *Significa*: calumniador
— *No significa*: traductor *(translator)*

TRAMP
— *Significa*: vagabundo
— *No significa*: trampa *(trap)*

TRANSCENDENTAL
— *Significa*: que trasciende; empírico confuso
— *No significa*: trascendental (importante) *(far-reaching)*

TREATMENT
— *Significa*: trato; tratamiento médico
— *No significa*: tratamiento (manera de nombrar a una persona) *(title, form of address)*

TUTOR
— *Significa*: profesor particular; preceptor
— *No significa*: tutor *(guardian)*

ULTIMATE
— *Significa*: definitivo
— *No significa*: último *(last, latest)*

ULTIMATELY
— *Significa*: finalmente
— *No significa*: últimamente *(lately)*

UNCONSCIOUS
— *Significa*: inconsciente (sin sentido)
— *No significa*: inconsciente (irresponsable) *(irresponsible)*

UNEDUCATED
— *Significa*: inculto
— *No significa*: maleducado *(rude, ill-mannered, impolite)*

URBANE
— *Significa*: urbano (cortés)
— *No significa*: urbano (de la ciudad, metropolitano) *(urban)*

VACANT
— *Significa*: vacante (adjetivo); distraído
— *No significa*: vacante (sustantivo) *(vacancy)*

VAGUE
— *Significa*: vago, impreciso
— *No significa*: vago (perezoso) *(lazy)*

VALOUR
— *Significa*: valor (coraje)
— *No significa*: valor (coste, sangre fría) *(value; nerve)*

VARIANCE
— *Significa*: desacuerdo
— *No significa*: variación *(variation)*

VASE
— *Significa*: jarrón
— *No significa*: vaso *(glass)*

VERSATILE
— *Significa*: de talentos o usos variados
— *No significa*: versátil *(changeable, inconstant)*

VICIOUS
— *Significa*: incorrecto
— *No significa*: vicioso *(depraved; addict)*

VIOLENT
— *Significa*: violento (con ímpetu e intensidad)
— *No significa*: violento (azorado) *(uncomfortable)*

VISITANT
— *Significa*: visitante de ultratumba
— *No significa*: visitante *(visitor)*

VISITATION
— *Significa*: visita religiosa
— *No significa*: visita *(visit)*

VOLUBILITY
— *Significa*: locuacidad
— *No significa*: volubilidad *(inconstancy)*

VOLUBLE
— *Significa*: locuaz
— *No significa*: voluble *(inconstant)*

VOTE
— *Significa*: voto (sufragio)
— *No significa*: voto (promesa) *(vow)*

VOYAGE
— *Significa*: travesía marítima
— *No significa*: viaje *(trip)*

VULGARIZE
— *Significa*: vulgarizar (convertir algo en una cosa de mal gusto)
— *No significa*: vulgarizar (hacer algo accesible al vulgo) *(to popularise)*

WAGON
— *Significa*: carreta
— *No significa*: vagón de tren *(railway car)*

Términos con acepciones comunes pero usados habitualmente en otro sentido

ABUSE
— *Significa*: insultar; insulto
— *También significa*: abusar; abuso

ACCESSORY
— *Significa*: cómplice
— *También significa*: accesorio

AFFECTION
— *Significa*: afecto
— *También significa*: afección

AGGRAVATE
— *Significa*: exasperar
— *También significa*: agravar, agravarse

ANTICIPATE
— *Significa*: prever
— *También significa:* anticipar

APOGEE
— *Significa*: apogeo astronómico
— *También significa:* apogeo

APOLOGY
— *Significa*: disculpa
— *También significa:* apología

APPARENT
— *Significa*: evidente
— *También significa:* aparente

APPARITION
— *Significa*: aparición fantasmal; visión de un ser
  sobrenatural
— *También significa:* acción y efecto de hacerse
  visible, aparecer

APPLICATION
— *Significa*: solicitud
— *También significa:* aplicación

APPLY
— *Significa*: destinar, solicitar
— *También significa:* aplicar

ASSUME
— *Significa*: suponer
— *También significa:* asumir

ATTEND
— *Significa*: asistir
— *También significa:* atender

CALLOUS
— *Significa*: insensible
— *También significa:* calloso

CASUAL
— *Significa*: informal, despreocupado
— *También significa:* casual

CHARACTER
— *Significa*: personaje
— *También significa:* carácter

CHEMIST
— *Significa*: farmacéutico (británico)
— *También significa*: químico

CIVIL
— *Significa*: cortés
— *También significa:* civil

CLERICAL
— *Significa*: administrativo
— *También significa:* clerical

COMMERCIAL
— *Significa*: anuncio
— *También significa:* comercial

COMMUNICATE
— *Significa*: comunicar
— *También significa:* comulgar; contagiar

CONCERN
— *Significa*: preocupación; empresa
— *También significa:* concernir

CONFOUND
— *Significa*: frustrar, maldecir
— *También significa:* confundir

CONSERVATORY
— *Significa*: invernadero
— *También significa:* conservatorio

CONSISTENT
— *Significa*: consistente
— *También significa:* consecuente, firme, constante

CONVENIENCE
— *Significa*: comodidad; ventaja
— *También significa:* conveniencia

DETERMINED
— *Significa*: resuelto, decidido
— *También significa:* determinado, fijo; establecido, concretado

DIRECTLY
— *Significa*: en seguida
— *También significa:* directamente

DISTINCT
— *Significa*: claro, visible
— *También significa:* distinto

DIVERT
— *Significa*: desviar
— *También significa:* divertir

ECONOMIST
— *Significa*: economista
— *También significa*: ahorrador

ENORMITY
— *Significa*: perversidad, atrocidad
— *También significa:* enormidad

EXALTED
— *Significa*: eminente; elevado
— *También significa:* exaltado (entusiasta, excitado)

EXCITED
— *Significa*: emocionado
— *También significa:* excitado

EXCITING
— *Significa*: emocionante
— *También significa:* excitante

EXTENSION
— *Significa*: prórroga
— *También significa:* extensión

EXTRAVAGANCE
— *Significa*: despilfarro
— *También significa:* extravagancia

FACILITIES
— *Significa*: medios (de transporte), instalaciones, servicios públicos
— *También significa:* facilidades

FIGURE
— *Significa*: cifra
— *También significa:* figura

GALLANT
— *Significa*: valiente
— *También significa:* galante

GOVERNESS
— *Significa*: institutriz
— *También significa:* gobernadora

GRADE
— *Significa*: nota, calificación
— *También significa:* grado, categoría, rango, jerarquía, clase

GUARDIAN
— *Significa*: guardián
— *También significa:* tutor

IMMATERIAL
— *Significa*: no importante
— *También significa:* inmaterial, abstracto, incorpóreo

IMMODEST
— *Significa*: impúdico
— *También significa:* inmodesto

IMPERTINENT
— *Significa*: improcedente, inoportuno
— *También significa:* impertinente

INDUSTRY
— *Significa*: industria
— *También significa:* laboriosidad

INEPT
— *Significa*: inoportuno
— *También significa:* inepto

INJURED
— *Significa*: herido
— *También significa:* injuriado

INJURIOUS
— *Significa*: dañino
— *También significa:* injurioso

INJURY
— *Significa*: herida
— *También significa:* injuria

INTERVENE
— *Significa*: transcribir
— *También significa:* intervenir

INTOXICATION
— *Significa*: borrachera
— *También significa:* intoxicación, envenenamiento; embriaguez, excitación

INTRODUCE
— *Significa*: presentar
— *También significa:* introducir, dar entrada a, meter, insertar

LABOUR
— *Significa*: trabajo, labor
— *También significa:* parto

MANIKIN
— *Significa*: enano
— *También significa:* maniquí

MASON
— *Significa*: albañil
— *También significa:* masón

MISERY
— *Significa*: aflicción, angustia
— *También significa:* miseria

MODEST
— *Significa*: modesto
— *También significa:* decente, decoroso, pudoroso; mesurado, módico

MODESTY
— *Significa*: modestia
— *También significa:* decencia

MOLEST
— *Significa*: abusar sexualmente
— *También significa:* molestar

MOVE
— *Significa*: trasladarse
— *También significa:* moverse

NERVE
— *Significa*: descaro, sangre fría
— *También significa:* nervio

NOTORIOUS
— *Significa*: de mala fama
— *También significa:* notorio

OBSCURE
— *Significa*: difícil de entender
— *También significa:* oscuro, falto de luz

OFFENSE
— *Significa*: delito grave
— *También significa:* ofensa

PAPER
— *Significa*: papel
— *También significa:* trabajo escrito

PARTIAL
— *Significa*: aficionado
— *También significa:* parcial

PATIENCE
— *Significa*: paciencia
— *También significa:* solitario (juego que ejecuta una sola persona, especialmente de naipes)

PECULIAR
— *Significa*: raro
— *También significa:* peculiar (particular, característico)

PREMISES
— *Significa*: local
— *También significa:* premisas

PRESENTLY
— *Significa*: inmediatamente
— *También significa:* en el momento presente

PRETEND
— *Significa*: fingir
— *También significa:* pretender

PRIVATE
— *Significa*: privado
— *También significa:* soldado raso

REALIZE
— *Significa*: darse cuenta
— *También significa*: realizar

RELATIVE
— *Significa*: pariente
— *También significa:* relativo

RESIGN
— *Significa*: dimitir
— *También significa:* resignarse

RETRACT
— *Significa*: retraerse
— *También significa:* retractarse

RICH
— *Significa*: rico
— *También significa:* pesado, fuerte, sabroso

SECULAR
— *Significa*: seglar
— *También significa:* secular

SERVANT
— *Significa*: sirviente
— *También significa:* funcionario

SIMPLE
— *Significa*: sencillo
— *También significa:* simple

SOLICITOUS
— *Significa*: ansioso, temeroso
— *También significa:* solícito

SPECTACLES
— *Significa*: espectáculos
— *También significa:* gafas

SUBJECT
— *Significa*: súbdito; tema, asignatura; expuesto, propenso
— *También significa:* sujeto

SUGGESTION
— *Significa*: sugerencia
— *También significa:* sugestión

VARIOUS
— *Significa*: variados
— *También significa:* varios

VERSATILE
— *Significa*: flexible (de múltiples usos y aplicaciones)
— *También significa:* versátil (variable); caprichoso, veleidoso

VILE
— *Significa*: vil
— *También significa:* asqueroso

Ejercicios

Ejercicio 1

Traduzca las siguientes frases al español.

1. Robert always assists his mother with the housework.
2. After we checked in at the reception desk, the porter took our luggage upstairs.
3. I want you all to be quiet.
4. If at first you don't succeed, try again.
5. The voyage from Brindisi to Corfu was rough.
6. Terry is rather voluble and he is not a good listener.
7. I can't record that old song.
8. The bomb exploded and killed three policemen.
9. Actually, I don't care whether you come or not.
10. He is a staunch adherent to the ideals of communism.
11. They removed all those products from the market.
12. He has a particular way of dealing with people.
13. The best part of the play was the argument between the male and the female protagonists.
14. There were many casualties during the war.
15. Peter went to a conference of Language School directors.
16. The conductor asked for our tickets but we had lost them.

17. They gave us directions to their house in the country.

18. I don't like drinking coffee out of a cup.

19. She wore a very conspicuous hat to the wedding.

20. He worked as an editor on the local newspaper for twenty five years.

21. He was looking for the exit but he couldn't find it.

22. There is a vase on the table.

23. Ted is a very gracious host.

24. Fran was dismayed when I asked for Mary's hand in marriage.

25. Al was embarrassed when I came to town.

26. I like the fabric they used to make that dress.

27. The principal doesn't think that young man is improvable.

28. As a boy he was known for his ingenuity.

29. There was a notice stating that there was no class on Monday.

30. I went to the library for a book.

31. He came up with a novel idea.

32. He made an extremely malign statement about his mother.

33. Daniel is an excellent physician.

34. Brian was preoccupied with his new-born child.

35. The teacher asked the students to repeat the refrain.

36. I have heard a lot of rumors around school.

37. Ringo was the sanest person in our family.

38. He is a true scholar.

39. His brother advised him where to go to college.
40. I feel alienated after the party last night.
41. He owns a very rare copy of Ulysses.
42. That word has several acceptations.
43. The president adverted to the crisis in Central America.
44. His secretary told him what was on the agenda.
45. He alternated between high society and poverty.
46. The announcer said that the product would soon be on the market.
47. I need an assistant at work.
48. We used to play in the attic when we were young.
49. After dinner he returned to the barracks.
50. She is a very candid person.

Ejercicio 2

Traduzca las siguientes frases al inglés.

1. Es un chico muy sensible.
2. El edificio tiene cabida para ochocientos escolares.
3. Hay que removerlo bien antes de usarlo.
4. Tenemos que resumir la novela.
5. Te la recomiendo porque es una academia seria.
6. (Él) Aprobó el examen sin estudiar.
7. El médico le pidió que aspirara.
8. Este año (ella) ha sacado unas calificaciones excelentes.

9. Te he prevenido de que llovería.
10. El abogado abandonó el juzgado furioso.
11. Le han adjudicado la casa.
12. Las potencias han acordado reunirse.
13. Mi profesor de español es muy simpático.
14. La vida social de un adolescente es tan importante como sus estudios.
15. La nuestra es una época de políticos versátiles.
16. Los monjes hacen voto de pobreza.
17. El jefe quería una relación de los empleados involucrados.
18. El médico ha reconocido a todos los afectados.
19. Han anunciado un polvo nuevo que quita las manchas sin mojar el tejido.
20. La apertura del sexto Festival de Jazz de San Francisco fue un éxito.
21. Estoy seguro de que es una trampa.
22. (Él) Tiene tendencia a usar tópicos.
23. Le han echado de la empresa por ser vago y llegar tarde.
24. Los bomberos han sofocado el incendio justo a tiempo.
25. De joven era escuálida.
26. Mi abuela guardaba siempre bajo la almohada una estampa de la Virgen.
27. El nuevo jefe del Departamento de Sanidad es una mujer.
28. Stephen era tan escandaloso que le pidieron que se fuera del bar.
29. Madeleine tiene mal genio.

30. Sus familiares no pueden testificar en su favor.

31. Nunca había experimentado una cosa tan extraña.

32. Yo creo que el marido de tu amiga es formal.

33. Los niños estaban muy exaltados cuando salieron del colegio.

34. Perdóname por llegar tarde, me entretuvo un viejo amigo.

35. Hay mucha gente cultivada que carece de buena educación.

36. Su vida (de él) está llena de desgracias.

37. Los artistas suelen demandar a las revistas por no respetar su intimidad.

38. Es un tema bastante corriente.

39. Alfred ha tenido mal genio desde que era una criatura.

40. Puede que no te sea simpático, pero es una persona consecuente.

41. Laureen fue una de las profesoras más comprensivas que tuve.

42. Si eres demasiado complaciente la gente te tomará el pelo.

43. Subimos al vagón de primera clase por equivocación.

44. Cada domingo vamos al campo.

45. (Ella) Terminó el bachillerato a los dieciséis años.

46. La comodidad es lo más importante en un tren.

47. Los dragones estaban hechos de cartón.

48. En Gran Bretaña se usa mucho el carbón.

49. Al padre le gustaba acostar a los niños.
50. Es muy difícil traducir chistes.

Ejercicio 3

Rellene los espacios en blanco con la(s) palabra(s) adecuadas(s).

1. In the 1970's there was an effort to
_____ classical music.

(vulgarize / divulge / populate / popularize)

2. The man he lived with was a _____ from the South of France.

(stranger / foreigner / estranger / neighbor)

3. What a _____ that you know each other!

(casualty / accident / coincidence / luck)

4. The statue we bought at the fair was made of
_____ .

(cartoon / carton / cardboard / box)

5. The _____ closed down by the police.

(locals were / local was / premise was / premises were)

6. Many people were waiting outside the Academy Awards ceremony to see the _____ .

(actors / artist / artist of cinema / arts)

7. I would like to meet your _____ from Spain.

(visitation / visitant / visit / visitor)

8. «His Highness» is the correct _____ when addressing the prince.

(treat / treatment / treatee / title)

9. I like some of their songs but there isn't much _____ in their music.

(variance / variety / various / verity)

10. Turn on the TV. I want to watch the _____ .

(notices / notes / news / informations)

11. Many great Greek thinkers were _____ of Socrates.

(experts / adepts / followers / sequins)

12. _____ are famous for building dams.

(Squirrels / Castors / Otters / Beavers)

13. The children want to watch the _____ .

(cartons / cartoons / animated drawings / drawings animated)

14. You can't trust that doctor. He is nothing but a _____ .

(talker / curia / curiator / charlatan)

15. He was one of the Bureau's most valuable men since he had important _____ in almost every country.

(confidents / confidence / confidants / confides)

16. He discovered the _____ to kill the senator.

(plot / conjuration / conjuror / plane)

17. She is such a valuable person that hiring her could only be _____ for the company.

(convenient / handy / confortable / beneficial)

18. Our house has three _____ .

(dormitories / sleeping rooms / bedrooms / habitations)

19. It was extremely _____ of them to ask for more money after what they had done.

(cynical / defaced / barefaced / scepticle)

20. They didn't know how long they would need help so they gave them a(n) _____ job.

(eventual / eventful / temporary / temporarily)

21. Most of the _____ of the terrorists were impossible.

(exigences / exigencies / demands / urgencies)

22. When he asked for his _____ the University officials could not find it anywhere.

(expedient / album / folder / record)

23. Drug abuse is a(n) _____ problem in the US.

(extended / widespread / disperse / extense)

24. We had planned to go on a picnic but it was raining so we went to a movie. When we came out it was sunny. In short, it was a rather _____ day.

(boring / fastidious / difficult / aggravating)

25. They had a beautiful picture of a _____ hillside.

(florished / florid / flower / flowery)

26. The artist had a(n) _____ of his latest work.

(exposition / exposé / exhibitioning / exhibition)

27. It was raining so I decided to wear my
_____ .

(gaberdine / raincoat / most of all / overalls)

28. We always _____ the mailman around Christmas.

(top / gratify / tip / propitiate)

29. Locking people up in cages is not a very _____ way of treating them.

(human / humane / humanish / humanoid)

30. I want you to _____ to stay off your right foot.

(intend / intent / try / procure)

31. After the accident, it took him a week before he could _____ .

(put himself sitting / incorporate / sit up / erect)

32. It is impolite to ask _____ questions.

(indiscrete / indiscreet / indescrit / indescrite)

33. He has _____ a lot of money in his son's education.

(invested / inverted / investment / inversion)

34. She has always been _____ of her older sister.

(invidious / inviable / envious / enviable)

35. I'm going down to the _____ to check a book out.

(library / book store / biblioteque / librettist)

36. She got terrible _____ on her report card.

(notes / grades / qualifications / levels)

37. I buy the _____ every day.

   (newspaper / news / periodical / revist)

38. He's a very important _____ in this town.

   (politic / policy / police / politician)

39. All bottles are _____ to assure cleanliness.

   (precincted / taped / sealed / singed)

40. She was a _____ bride.

   (priceless / precious / beautiful / bountiful)

41. He _____ to the others that he had killed over one hundred bears.

   (boasted / jacked / presumed / agreed)

42. He had a job handing out _____ to passers-by.

   (prospects / follets / leaflets / leaves)

43. His mother asked him if he wanted to _____ the butter.

   (prove / comprise / taste / toss)

44. After attempting many times to convince her, he had to _____ to drastic measures.

   (recur / record / resort / recollect)

45. The discovery of America was one of the most _____ events in history.

   (adequate / relevant / outstanding / relieving)

46. Before writing a composition it is wise to write a (an) _____ .

   (theme / scheme / outline / headline)

47. I can't _____ this hot weather for very long.

   (resist / support / aguant / endure)

48. I have to go to a faculty _____ on Friday night.

(encounter / meeting / manifestation / reunion)

49. The police have detained four _____ .

(suspects / suspicious / suspecters / suspicons)

50. He didn't study so it's not suprising that he _____ .

(fell / failed / fractured / suspended)

Términos con correspondencias múltiples

Algunos términos españoles corresponden a varios términos en inglés. Es decir, encontramos una única palabra en español para varias representaciones en inglés, que responden a diferentes acepciones o fragmentos del campo semántico de ésta. Por ejemplo, al término *ahogarse* español corresponden dos palabras inglesas: *to drown*, si se trata de ahogarse en el agua y *to choke*, si significa asfixiarse.

A continuación, ofrecemos una completa relación de correspondencias de este tipo, las más habituales.

AHOGAR, AHOGARSE
— *to drown* (en agua)
　He drowned because he could not swim.
　Se ahogó porque no sabía nadar.
— *to choke* (asfixiar, asfixiarse)
　He choked on a chicken bone.
　Se ahogó con un hueso de pollo.

APRENDER
— *to learn* (+ sustantivo)
  I am learning French.
  Estoy aprendiendo francés.
— *to learn how to* (+ infinitivo)
  I learned how to ride a bike when I was five.
  Aprendí a montar en bicicleta cuando tenía cinco años.

APROBAR
— *to approve of* (estar conforme)
  I don't approve of that action.
  No apruebo esa acción.
— *to approve* (dar el visto bueno, autorizar)
  The mayor approved the plan.
  El alcalde aprobó el plan.
— *to pass* (superar un examen)
  I passed all of my exams.
  He aprobado todos los exámenes.

ASISTIR
— *to attend* (estar presente)
  He attended class regularly.
  Asistía a clase con regularidad.
— *to assist* (ayudar, atender)
  The nurse assisted her in her recovery.
  La enfermera la asistió durante su recuperación.

BANCO
— *bank* (establecimiento financiero)

I keep my money in the same bank as my mother.
Tengo el dinero en el mismo banco que mi madre.
— *bench* (asiento)
We sat on a bench in the park.
Nos sentamos en un banco del parque.

CADA
— *each* (de uno en uno)
They cost a dollar each.
Valen un dólar cada uno.
— *every* (todos)
I walk to school every day.
Cada día voy andando al colegio.

CARNE
— *meat* (comestible)
He is a vegetarian. He doesn't eat meat.
Es vegetariano, no come carne.
— *flesh* (no comestible)
The cut was so deep you could see the flesh.
El corte era tan profundo que se veía la carne.

CARRERA
— *race* (competición)
He has never lost a race.
No ha perdido nunca una carrera.
— *career* (profesional)
Nothing is more important to him than his career.
Para él no hay nada más importante que su carrera.

— *major, lied of study* (universitaria)
You have hundreds of majors to choose from at Berkeley.
En Berkeley tienes cientos de carreras para escoger.

CERO
— *zero* (cifra)
One million is a one with six zeroes.
Un millón es un uno con seis ceros.
— *O* (números de teléfono)
My number is four-two-three-six-o-nine-one.
Mi número es cuatro, dos, tres, seis, cero, nueve, uno.
— *nil* (nada; deportes)
They moved their business and reduced their overhead to almost nil.
Trasladaron el negocio y redujeron los gastos generales casi a cero.
They won three to nil.
Ganaron tres a cero.

CLIENTE
— *client* (de profesionales)
All of my lawyer's clients are rich widows.
Todos los clientes de mi abogado son viudas ricas.
— *customer* (de empresas, tiendas)
A store must please its customers.
Las tiendas deben procurar complacer a sus clientes.

Cobrar

— *to cash* (un cheque)
   I cashed the check yesterday.
   Cobré el cheque ayer.
— *to charge* (por un servicio o mercancía)
   He charges twenty dollars an hour to clean your house.
   Cobra veinte dólares la hora por limpiarte la casa.
— *to collect* (una deuda)
   If you don't collect the money soon, he'll never pay you.
   Si no cobras pronto, no te pagará nunca.
— *to make* (en un empleo)
   He makes fifty thousand dollars a year.
   Cobra cincuenta mil dólares al año.

Cocina

— *kitchen* (habitación)
   I often eat in the kitchen.
   Suelo comer en la cocina.
— *stove* (instrumento)
   We need a new stove. The old one is broken.
   Necesitamos una cocina nueva, la vieja está rota.
   cuisine (artes culinarias)
   I have a good book on Mexican cuisine.
   Tengo un buen libro de cocina mexicana.

Como

— *like* (+ sustantivo o pronombre)

He wants to be like his father.
Quiere ser como su padre.

— *as* (+ verbo)
As you know, he is very intelligent.
Como sabes, es muy inteligente.

— *as* (+ sustantivo)
As a teacher, I feel it is necessary to improve the present evaluation system.
Como maestro, considero que es necesario mejorar el actual sistema de evaluación.

— *as* (comparación)
He is not as tall as his father.
No es tan alto como su padre.

— *how* (adverbio interrogativo)
How is he?
¿Cómo está?

— *what* (preguntas sobre la personalidad y la apariencia)
What is he like?
¿Cómo es? (personalidad)
What does he look like?
¿Cómo es? (apariencia)

CONDUCIR
— *to drive* (vehículo)
She wants to learn how to drive.
Quiere aprender a conducir.

— *to lead* (guiar, llevar por el camino debido)
All roads lead to Rome.
Todos los caminos conducen a Roma.

CONFERENCIA
— *lecture* (de un orador)
He gave a lecture on Global economy.
Dio una conferencia sobre economía mundial.
— *conference* (reunión para celebrar una conversación)
He was the only representative of his country at the conference of Western nations.
Era el único representante de su país en la conferencia de naciones occidentales.

CONOCER
— *to know* (tener informacion)
I know Jim very well.
Conozco muy bien a Jim.
— *to get to know* (adquirir información)
We got to know each other better in the two weeks we spent together.
Nos conocimos mejor durante las dos semanas que pasamos juntos.
— *to meet* (por primera vez a personas)
I met him twenty years ago.
Lo conocí hace veinte años.

CONTAR
— *to tell* (cuentos, chistes, mentiras)
He told a joke to cheer her up.
Contó un chiste para animarla.
— *to count* (números)
He only knows how to count to ten.
Sólo sabe contar hasta diez.

CREER
— *to think/believe* (creer que)
  I think/believe that he did it.
  Creo que lo hizo él.
— *to believe* (creer en)
  I believe in God.
  Creo en Dios.

CUALQUIERA
— *either* (de dos)
  Either of you will do.
  Cualquiera de vosotros servirá.
— *any* (de más de dos)
  Take any of them.
  Coge cualquiera.

CHIMENEA
— *fireplace* (interior)
  We have a fireplace in our bedroom.
  Tenemos una chimenea en el dormitorio.
— *chimney* (exterior)
  Santa Claus enters the house through the chimney.
  Santa Claus entra en casa por la chimenea.

DECIR
— *to say* (sin objeto indirecto)
  He said his name.
  Dijo su nombre.
— *to tell* (con objeto indirecto)
  He told me his name.

Me dijo su nombre.
— *to tell* (la verdad, una mentira, un cuento, la hora)
   He always tells the truth.
   Siempre dice la verdad.

DEJAR

— *to let/allow* (permitir)
   He let me drive his car.
   Me dejó conducir su coche.
— *to lend* (prestar)
   He lent me five dollars.
   Me dejó cinco dólares.
— *to leave* (salir de)
   He left the city at dawn.
   Dejó la ciudad al amanecer.
— *to stop* + gerundio (dejar de + infinitivo)
   He never stops crying.
   No deja nunca de llorar.
— *to fail* (omitir)
   Don't fail to visit the Picasso Museum.
   No dejes de ir al Museo Picasso.

DESPEDIR

— *to say goodbye* (decir adiós)
   He said goodbye with tears in his eyes.
   Se despidió con lágrimas en los ojos.
— *to see off* (acompañar a una estación, un aeropuerto, etc.)
   Tim saw his nephew off at the airport.
   Tim despidió a su sobrino en el aeropuerto.

— *to fire* (del trabajo)
My boss fired me for coming late.
Mi jefe me despidió por llegar tarde.

DIRIGIR, DIRIGIRSE
— *to address* (hablar a alguien)
I was surprised when the old Greek fisherman addressed me in English.
Me sorprendió que el viejo pescador griego se dirigiera a mí en inglés.
— *to head for* (ir hacia)
After traveling around the world for two years he headed for home.
Después de viajar por todo el mundo durante dos años, se dirigió a casa.
— *to conduct* (una orquesta)
Conducting an orchestra demands a lot of concentration.
Dirigir una orquesta exige mucha concentración.
— *to point* (apuntar)
He pointed the telescope toward Mars.
Dirigió el telescopio hacia Marte.
— *to run/manage* (gobernar, administrar)
His father tought him how to run the company before he died.
Su padre le enseñó a dirigir la empresa antes de morir.
— *to direct* (películas)
He directed Paul Newman's latest film.
Dirigió la última película de Paul Newman.

ENCONTRAR
— *to find* (hallar)
  I haven't found an apartment yet.
  Todavía no he encontrado piso.
— *to meet* (concurrir en un lugar predeterminado)
  We'll meet on the bridge.
  Nos encontraremos en el puente.
— *to run into* (coincidir en un lugar casualmente)
  I ran into Bob on the bus today.
  Hoy me he encontrado a Bob en el autobús.

ENSEÑAR
— *to teach* (+ sustantivo)
  I teach English.
  Enseño inglés.
— *to teach how to* (+ infinitivo)
  I taught her how to swim.
  Le enseñé a nadar.
— *to show* (mostrar)
  I showed her a picture of myself when I was little.
  Le enseñé una foto de cuando era pequeño.
— *to show how to* (hacer una demostración)
  I showed her how to iron a shirt.
  Le enseñé cómo se plancha una camisa.

ESPERAR
— *to hope* (tener esperanza)
  I hope you come.
  Espero que vengas.
— *to expect* (esperar con seguridad)

I am expecting him at ten past seven.
Lo espero a las siete y diez.
— *to wait for* (aguardar)
Mary was late so I had to wait for half an hour.
Mary llegó con retraso y tuve que esperar media
hora.

EXPERIMENTAR
— *to experience* (sentir)
I have never experienced such humiliation.
Nunca he experimentado tal humillación.
— *to experiment* (someter a prueba)
First he experimented with mice.
Primero experimentó con ratones.

FALTAR
— *to be missing* (no encontrarse presente)
*When Stephen got to the station there was a bag
missing.*
Cuando Stephen llegó a la estación, le faltaba una
maleta.
— *to need* (necesitar)
I need three more stamps to have the entire collection.
Me faltan tres sellos para terminar la colección.
— *to lack* (carecer)
*He lacks the necessary discipline to become a great
pianist.*
Le falta la disciplina necesaria para ser un gran
pianista.
— *in* (tiempo)

In five minutes they will open.
Faltan cinco minutos para que abran.

FUENTE
— *spring* (manantial)
   The water from the spring came out as cold as ice.
   El agua de la fuente salía fría como el hielo.
— *fountain* (artificial)
   In Madrid there are fountains everywhere.
   En Madrid hay fuentes por todas partes.
— *source* (procedencia)
   Money is the source of all evil.
   El dinero es la fuente de toda maldad.
— *platter* (bandeja)
   The waiter brought a platter of vegetables.
   El camarero nos trajo una fuente de verduras.

GANAR
— *to earn/make* (dinero con el trabajo)
   He doesn't earn/make much money.
   No gana mucho dinero.
— *to win* (dinero en el juego)
   He won five hundred dollars at the races.
   Ganó quinientos dólares en las carreras.
— *to win* (competición)
   They won the match.
   Ganaron el partido.
— *to beat* (derrotar)
   They beat them by three points.
   Los ganaron por tres puntos.

GUARDAR
— *to save* (reservar)
Save me a piece of cake.
Guárdame un trozo de pastel.
— *to guard* (proteger)
The soldier had to guard the warehouse.
El soldado tenía que guardar el almacén.

HABLAR
— *to talk to/with* (con una persona informalmente)
We talked for hours about old times.
Hablamos durante horas de los viejos tiempos.
— *to speak to/with* (con una persona formalmente)
I spoke to him about his daughter.
Le hablé de su hija.
— *to speak* (una lengua)
He spoke German and Spanish.
Hablaba alemán y español.
— *to talk* (*nonsense*, de tonterías; *business*, de negocios; *shop*, del trabajo)
Whenever they get together they talk shop.
Cuando se reúnen hablan siempre del trabajo.

HACER
— *to do* (actividades o trabajos)
I don't like doing any kind of work.
No me gusta hacer ningún tipo de trabajo.
— *to do*, en las expresiones:
to do business (hacer negocios)
to do a favor (hacer un favor)

to do good (hacer bien)
to do harm (hacer mal)
to do one's best (hacer todo lo posible)
— to make (fabricar, crear, construir)
  Do you know how to make cakes?
  ¿Sabes hacer pasteles?
— to make, en las expresiones:
  to make the bed (hacer la cama)
  to make an effort (hacer un esfuerzo)
  to make a noise (hacer ruido)
  to make peace (hacer las paces)

HISTORIA
— story (relato)
  My father told me the story of how he became famous.
  Mi padre me contó la historia de cómo se hizo famoso.
— history (sucesión de hechos pasados: ciencia que los estudia)
  Humankind has progressed throughout history.
  La humanidad ha ido progresando a lo largo de la historia.

INVITAR
— to invite (formal)
  We were invited to the wedding.
  Nos invitaron a la boda.
— to ask (informal)
  I asked her to go to the movies.
  La invité al cine.

LADRÓN

— *thief* (sin violencia)
 He was a thief when he was a young boy.
 De muchacho era ladrón.
— *burglar* (que entra en una casa o establecimiento por la noche)
 The burglar made a hole in the wall.
 El ladrón hizo un agujero en la pared.
— *robber* (con violencia o amenaza de violencia)
 The robber told them to put their hands up.
 El ladrón les mandó poner las manos en alto.

LLEVAR

— *to carry* (transportar)
 She carried the baby in her arms.
 Llevaba al niño en brazos.
— *to take* (de aquí allí)
 He took the car to the garage.
 Llevó el coche al taller.
— *to take away* (llevarse de aquí o de allí)
 Take this ashtray away from here.
 Llévate este cenicero de aquí.
— *to wear* (puesto)
 He always wears a hat.
 Siempre lleva sombrero.

MARCA

— *make* (vehículos a motor)
 What make is your car?
 ¿De qué marca es tu coche?

— *brand* (todo lo demás)
Anne likes a very expensive brand of perfume.
A Ana le gusta una marca muy cara de perfume.
— *mark* (señal)
He made a mark on all his things to identify them.
Puso una marca en todas sus cosas para identificarlas.

Más
— *more* (comparación)
He has more money than his friend.
Tiene más dinero que su amigo.
— *plus* (sumas)
Seven plus eight equals fifteen.
Siete más ocho son quince.
— *over* (que rebasa un límite)
It took him over two hours to finish the exam.
Tardó más de dos horas en terminar el examen.
— *better* (con «like»)
That sweater is more expensive but I like this one better.
Ese suéter es más caro pero éste me gusta más.

Matrimonio
— *marriage* (institución)
Marriage is a very serious affair.
El matrimonio es un asunto muy serio.
— *a married couple* (una pareja casada)
A married couple came to the hotel and asked for a room.

Entró un matrimonio al hotel y preguntó si tenían habitaciones.

MENOS
— *less* (comparativo con sustantivos no contables, adjetivos y verbos)
I have less money now than yesterday.
Ahora tengo menos dinero que ayer.
He is infinitely less intelligent than his brother.
Es infinitamente menos inteligente que su hermano.
He drinks less than he used to.
Bebe menos que antes.
— *fewer* (comparativo con sustantivos contables)
She has fewer brothers than I do.
Tiene menos hermanos que yo.
— *but/except* (salvo)
Everyone went to the party except me.
Todo el mundo fue a la fiesta menos yo.
— *minus* (restas)
Seven minus three equals four.
Siete menos tres son cuatro.

MIRAR
— *to look*
Look into my eyes.
Mírame a los ojos.
— *to watch* (algo en movimiento)
I watch TV every night.
Cada noche miro la televisión.

— *to stare* (fijamente)
All of the students stared at the new girl when she walked into the classroom.
Todos los alumnos se quedaron mirando a la muchacha nueva cuando entró en la clase.
— *to gaze* (con asombro)
She gazed at the stranger walking into her party.
Miró con asombro al extraño que entraba en su fiesta.
— *to glare* (con ira)
She glared at the waiter who had spilled the soup on her.
Miró airadamente al camarero que le había echado la sopa encima.
— *to face* (estar orientado)
The house faces the East.
La casa mira al este.

NINGUNO
— *neither* (de dos)
Neither of you is old enough.
Ninguno de los dos tenéis edad suficiente.
— *None* (de más de dos)
None of the students understood.
Ninguno de los alumnos lo entendió.
— *any* (en frase negativa)
Would you give me a cigarette? I don't have any left.
¿Me das un cigarrillo? Ya no me queda ninguno.

OCUPADO
— *busy* (atareado)
I am very busy at work now.
Estoy muy ocupado en el trabajo.
— *occupied* (no vacante)
The toilet was occupied when she arrived.
Cuando llegó, el servicio estaba ocupado.
— *taken* (asiento)
Is this seat taken?
¿Está ocupado este asiento?

ORILLA
— *shore* (mar)
They rowed to shore from the ship.
Remaron hasta la orilla desde el barco.
— *bank* (río)
They built a house on the bank of the Mississippi.
Construyeron una casa a orillas del Mississippi.

PAGAR
— *to pay* (dinero o facturas)
I paid him the five hundred and twenty dollars that I owed him.
Le pagué los quinientos veinte dólares que le debía.
I paid the gas bill.
He pagado la factura del gas.
— *to pay for* (objetos y servicios)
I paid for lunch.
La comida la pagué yo.

PAR
—*pair* (inseparable)
  She was wearing a pair of red socks.
  Llevaba un par de calcetines rojos.
—*couple* (separable)
  He came home with a couple of friends.
  Vino a casa con un par de amigos.

PARECER, PARECERSE
—*to seem* (causar una impresión)
  You seem tired.
  Pareces cansado.
—*to look like* (semejanza de una cosa a otra)
  You look like your father.
  Te pareces a tu padre.
—*to look alike* (semejanza entre dos cosas)
  Arnold and Fred look alike.
  Arnold y Fred se parecen.

PARTIDO
—*game* (de béisbol, de baloncesto y de fútbol americano)
  It was the longest basketball game I had ever seen.
  Fue el partido de baloncesto más largo que había visto en mi vida.
—*match* (de otros deportes)
  The boys are not here because they went to the soccer match.
  Los chicos no están porque se han ido al partido de fútbol.

PASAR, PASARSE

— *to pass* (acercar, alargar una cosa)
Pass me the salt, please.
Pásame la sal, por favor.

— *to pass* (adelantar)
He passed the car on the right.
Pasó al coche por la derecha.

— *to pass* (superar una prueba)
He passed the exam in June.
Pasó el examen en junio.

— *to pass/to be taken for* (ser confundido con)
Phillip could be taken for a French boy.
Phillip podría pasar por francés.

— *to go by* (ir)
After the party we'll go by your house.
Después de la fiesta pasaremos por tu casa.

— *to go by* (transcurrir)
Five years have already gone by since I arrived.
Ya han pasado cinco años desde que llegué.

— *to go through* (atravesar por el interior)
The train goes through a tunnel after it leaves the town.
El tren pasa por un túnel a la salida del pueblo.

— *to spend* (períodos de tiempo)
He spent five years in Mexico.
Pasó cinco años en México.

— *to happen* (ocurrir)
The accident happened in Monterrey.
El accidente pasó en Monterrey.

— *to be over* (haber terminado)

The most difficult part of your life is over.
Ya ha pasado el período más difícil de tu vida.
— *to get by* (arreglárselas)
She couldn't get by without my help.
No podría pasar sin mi ayuda.
— *to turn* (las hojas de un libro)
I wasn't reading, I was just turning the pages.
No leía, sólo pasaba las páginas.
— *to get over* (recuperarse)
You'll get over your illness soon.
Pronto se te pasará la enfermedad.
— *to go bad* (echarse a perder)
The oranges went bad because we left them out too long.
Las naranjas se pasaron porque las dejamos fuera demasiado tiempo.
— *to go too far/to overdo* (excederse)
The boys should have fun but sometimes they go too far.
Los chicos deben divertirse, pero a veces se pasan.
— *to miss* (no aprovechar)
You missed your chance to see the most beautiful woman in the world.
Se te ha pasado la oportunidad de ver a la mujer más guapa del mundo.

PASEO
— *walk* (una vuelta)
I enjoy going for walks in the park.
Me gusta dar paseos por el parque.

— *promenade* (marítimo)
Sitges has a lovely promenade.
Sitges tiene un precioso paseo marítimo.
— *boulevard* (calle ancha)
Madrid is known for its wide boulevards.
Madrid es famoso por sus amplios paseos.

PENSAR
— *to think* (usar la capacidad mental)
He only thinks about his girlfriend.
Sólo piensa en su novia.
— *to intend* (tener intención)
I intend to retire at forty-five.
Pienso retirarme a los cuarenta y cinco años.

PEQUEÑO
— *small* (tamaño reducido)
That house is too small for us.
Esa casa es demasiado pequeña para nosotros.
— *little* (en sentido emotivo)
That's a cute little house.
Es una casita bonita.
— *little* (comparación)
The little hand of a clock.
La aguja pequeña de un reloj.
My little brother.
Mi hermano pequeño.

PERDER
— *to lose* (no saber dónde está)
I lost my sweater.

He perdido el suéter.

— *to lose* (salir derrotado)
We lost the game.
Perdimos el partido.

— *to miss* (no coincidir en el tiempo)
I missed the bus to Santa Barbara.
He perdido el autobús de Santa Bárbara.

— *to waste* (desaprovechar)
He wasted his time looking for the perfect woman.
Perdió el tiempo buscando a la mujer perfecta.

PERSONA

— *person* (singular)
You are the only person I know here.
Eres la única persona que conozco aquí.

— *people* (plural)
The three people in the corner are my cousins.
Las tres personas de la esquina son mis primos.

PISO

— *apartment* (vivienda)
He bought a five-room apartment for his son.
Le compró un piso de cinco habitaciones a su hijo.

— *floor* (planta)
What floor do you live on?
¿En qué piso vive?

— *story* (altura)
She lives in a twenty-storied apartment building.
Vive en un edificio de veinte pisos.

PLATO
— *plate/dish* (recipiente)
   Would you please put the plates on the table?
   ¿Quieres poner los platos en la mesa, por favor?
— *dish* (cantidad de comida preparada)
   Macaroni and cheese is my favourite dish.
   Los macarrones con queso son mi plato favorito.
— *course* (una de las partes de la comida)
   They served a five-course dinner at the wedding.
   En la boda sirvieron una cena de cinco platos.

POLÍTICA
— *politics* (gobierno estatal)
   They never talk about politics.
   No hablan nunca de política.
— *policy* (estrategia o norma)
   They have been accused of having no foreign policy.
   Se les ha acusado de no tener política exterior.

PONERSE
— *to put on* (vestirse)
   He put on his shoes slowly.
   Se puso los zapatos despacio.
— *to start* (iniciar una actividad)
   She started reading as soon as she got on the bus.
   Se puso a leer en cuanto subió al autobús.

PRONTO
— *early* (al principio)
   We always get up early.

Siempre nos levantamos pronto.
— *soon* (al cabo de poco tiempo)
If you want to wait, David will be here soon.
Si quieres esperar, David llegará pronto.

PUBLICIDAD
— *advertising* (comercial)
Advertising is what sells a product.
La publicidad es lo que hace que se venda un producto.
— *publicity* (no comercial)
Her marriage received a lot of publicity.
Su matrimonio tuvo mucha publicidad.
— *propaganda* (política, religiosa)
There has been a lot of propaganda about the rescue of the hostages.
Se ha hecho mucha publicidad del rescate de los rehenes.

PÚBLICO
— *public* (gente en general)
The office opens to the public at nine o'clock.
La oficina abre al público a las nueve.
— *audience* (de un espectáculo o programa)
The audience applauded for twenty minuts straight.
El público aplaudió veinte minutos seguidos.

RECORDAR
— *to remember* (tener en la mente)
I'm sorry, I don't remember your name.

Lo siento, no recuerdo tu nombre.

— *to remind* (hacer recordar)
Remind me to call my mother at six o'clock.
Recuérdame que llame a mi madre a las seis.

— *to remind of* (sugerir una asociacion)
That song reminds me of my school years.
Esa canción me recuerda mis años de estudiante.

RECUERDO

— *souvenir* (objeto o regalo destinado a recordar un lugar o suceso)
We bought so many souvenirs in Paris that they did not fit in our suitcase.
Compramos tantos recuerdos en París que no nos cabían en la maleta.

— *memento* (objeto que hace recordar a una persona o suceso emotivo)
She gave him a ring as a memento of their relationship.
Le regaló un anillo como recuerdo de sus relaciones.

— *regards* (saludos)
Give my regards to your family.
Dale recuerdos a tu familia.

— *memory* (del pasado)
I have fond memories of my childhood.
Tengo recuerdos entrañables de mi niñez.

RELOJ

— *watch* (de pulsera o bolsillo)
I don't wear a watch.

Nunca llevo reloj.
— *clock* (de pared, de sobremesa, de pie)
We are looking for a kitchen clock.
Estamos buscando un reloj de cocina.

ROBAR
— *to rob* (a personas)
They robbed me in broad daylight.
Me robaron a plena luz del día.
— *to steal* (cosas)
They stole my wallet, my overcoat and my watch on the bus.
Me robaron la cartera, el abrigo y el reloj en el autobús.

SALIR
— *to go out* (para divertirse)
I like going out at night.
Me gusta salir por la noche.
— *to go out* (tener relaciones)
Shawn goes out with an old friend of mine.
Shawn sale con una vieja amiga mía.
— *to leave* (irse)
He left the country immediately.
Salió inmediatamente del país.

SEGURO
— *sure/certain* (con certeza)
I'm sure he'll be successful one day.
Estoy seguro de que algún día tendrá éxito.

—*safe* (sin peligro)
  It's always safer to walk against the traffic.
  Siempre es más seguro andar en dirección contraria al tráfico.
—*insurance* (póliza)
  If you use a credit card to pay for your flight they give you life insurance.
  Si usas la tarjeta de crédito para pagar el billete de avión te regalan un seguro de vida.

SITIO
—*place* (punto en el espacio)
  They always meet at the same place.
  Siempre se encuentran en el mismo sitio.
—*room* (espacio)
  We need more room for the books.
  Necesitamos más sitio para los libros.

SOMBRA
—*shade* (donde no da el sol)
  Let's find a table in the shade.
  Busquemos una mesa a la sombra.
—*shadow* (silueta proyectada por un cuerpo)
  The shadow of the tree looked like a person.
  La sombra del árbol parecía una persona.

SUSPENDER
—*to suspend* (colgar)
  A piñata is suspended from a branch or crossbeam.
  Las piñatas se suspenden de una rama o viga.

— *to call off* (interrumpir)
The game was called off because of the rain.
Suspendieron el partido a causa de la lluvia.
— *to fail* (no pasar un examen)
*He failed his final exam and he will have to take it
again.*
Suspendió el examen final y tendrá que hacerlo
otra vez.

TIERRA
— *Earth* (planeta)
Earth is the third planet from the Sun.
La Tierra es el tercer planeta del Sol.
— *earth/soil* (donde crecen las plantas)
*You must have good earth if you want your plants to
grow.*
Para que crezcan las plantas hay que tener tierra
de calidad.
— *ground* (superficie)
It rained a lot but the ground soaked it all up.
Llovió mucho pero la tierra lo absorbió todo.
— *land* (lo que no es mar ni aire)
We haven't seen land in two months.
Hace dos meses que no vemos tierra.
— *land* (parcela)
He owns some land in Alaska.
Tiene algo de tierra en Alaska.
— *land* (división territorial)
California is a land of contrasts.
California es tierra de contrastes.

TODO
— *all/the whole* (adjetivos)
  I have been waiting for you all morning.
  Llevo esperándote toda la mañana.
  I have been waiting for you the whole morning.
— *everything* (pronombre)
  I like everything.
  Me gusta todo.

TRABAJO
— *job* (contable)
  He has a good job.
  Tiene un buen trabajo.
— *work* (no contable)
  It is not easy to find work these days.
  Hoy en día no es fácil encontrar trabajo.
— *employment* (no contable culto)
  I sent the forms to the Ministry of Employment.
  Envié los impresos al Ministerio de Trabajo.

TRATAR
— *to try* (procurar)
  I tried to convince him.
  Traté de convencerlo.
— *to treat* (bien o mal)
  He treated his children like pets.
  Trataba a sus hijos como animales domésticos.
— *to deal with* (asuntos)
  The movie deals with problems in the city.
  La película trata de los problemas de la ciudad.

ÚLTIMO

— *last* (que no tiene sucesión)
  John was the last person to come in.
  John fue el último en entrar.
— *latest* (hasta el momento)
  Have you heard Wonder's latest album?
  Has oído el último disco de Wonder?

VIAJE

— *trip* (ida de un sitio a otro)
  He went on a business trip for two weeks.
  Estuvo dos semanas de viaje de negocios.
— *journey* (por tierra de considerable distancia)
  The book talks about his journey to Russia.
  El libro habla de su viaje a Rusia.
— *voyage* (travesía marítima)
  I'd love to take a long sea voyage.
  Me encantaría hacer un largo viaje por mar.
— *travels* (andanzas prolongadas por el mundo)
  During his travels he met a lot of people.
  Durante sus viajes conoció a mucha gente.

VOLVER

— *to go back* (de aquí allí)
  «You should go back home», said his best friend.
  Deberías volver a casa —dijo su mejor amigo.
— *to come back* (de allí aquí)
  «You should come back home», said his mother.
  Deberías volver a casa —dijo su madre.
  to return (en ambas direcciones)

Ejercicios

Ejercicio 4

Traduzca las frases siguientes al inglés.

1. Recuerdo cuando eras joven y feliz.
2. Tienes que vivir en un país para llegar a conocerlo bien.
3. (Él) Es más inteligente de lo que parece.
4. (Ella)Es muy buena persona.
5. Los mayores tienen menos paciencia.
6. ¿Te ha contado alguna vez la historia de cómo se hizo famoso?
7. ¿Has pagado el recibo del teléfono?
8. Si piensas antes de actuar te equivocarás menos.
9. Enseña matemáticas a niños de seis años.
10. Aprendió el español cuando tenía doce años.
11. Perdí tu libro.
12. Te guardaré el sitio.
13. El médico me miró el dedo del pie.
14. No estoy seguro de si quiere venir o no.
15. Necesito un par de guantes de piel.
16. La publicidad televisiva es muy cara.
17. En Roma hay miles de tiendas de recuerdos.
18. No puedo llevar reloj mientras trabajo.
19. Quiere un trabajo en un periódico.
20. No apruebo el comportamiento de tu hermana.
21. Suspendieron el juicio a causa de la ausencia de uno de los abogados.

22. Debes cobrar los cheques de viaje en cuanto llegues.

23. Están ustedes invitados a un almuerzo con el gobernador.

24. El policía le dijo al niño que debería volver a casa.

25. Ninguno de los dos caminos conducía al sur.

26. Cualquiera de esos dos sombreros te irá bien.

27. Se pone perfume cada día.

28. Mi padre me dejó ir al cine con Pablo y David.

29. Dejó de fumar hace cuatro años.

30. Es un arquitecto con clientes muy especiales.

31. Hicimos un viaje a Venecia para asistir al festival de cine.

32. Tienen una cocina enorme.

33. El público no entenderá sus razones.

34. Soy uno de los clientes más regulares de esta librería.

35. El rey es como cualquier otra persona.

36. ¿Cómo es el rey? (personalidad).

37. Los hindúes inventaron el cero.

38. Pareces aburrido.

39. Tuve que trabajar todo el fin de semana.

40. Gana mucho más dinero que yo.

41. No me gusta despedirme.

42. En este barrio te juzgan según la marca de tu coche.

43. Tenemos un piso en la costa.

44. Yo fui el último en verlo.

45. Yo no creo en el matrimonio.

46. Los extraterrestres no querían bajar a la Tierra.
47. El Papa se dirigió a la gente en seis idiomas.
48. Espero que mañana no llueva.
49. La política es una de las profesiones más privilegiadas.
50. Creo que te equivocas.

Ejercicio 5

Corrija las siguientes frases si hace falta.

1. They own a very expensive car. I don't know what brand.
2. The fountain of a river is where it begins.
3. We walked along the walk for hours.
4. He went out of the country to get a visa.
5. I passed three weeks with him.
6. You have to do more than assist class.
7. He said me he would come at seven.
8. He talks French like a native.
9. She drowned on her sandwich.
10. My mother always does us cakes for our birthdays.
11. He has experimented the most terrible pain you can imagine.
12. The man with the beard, the black hat and the long coat robbed my wallet.
13. We couldn't find any shadow on the beach.
14. You should get going early if you want to catch the train that leaves in half an hour.

15. I knew him for the first time when I was ten.
16. You remember me of a teacher I had in grammar school.
17. Twelve more ten equals twenty two.
18. Persons are very strange.
19. The less brothers and sisters you have, the more presents you get.
20. He paid the dress with his own money.
21. He thought to leave at eight o'clock.
22. You lost your mother. She left a moment ago.
23. We don't have enough place for a table in the kitchen.
24. I see TV three hours a days.
25. It isn't a very sure neighborhood.
26. I only have a pair of dollars.
27. We bought a watch to hang on the wall in the kitchen.
28. He has approved all of his exams this year.
29. He suspended all of his exams last year.
30. Neither of my three sisters is married.
31. On a basketball team either player can take the ball out.
32. She always carries very strange hats.
33. He let me twenty-five dollars until the end of the month.
34. When we were in Macy's, ninety per cent of the clients were over eighty years old.
35. The travel from New York to San Francisco takes fifty eight hours.
36. Do you have a gas or electric kitchen?

37. I like going to concerts just to look at the public.
38. How a tax-payer, I have the right to know what the money is spent on.
39. He doesn't really look alike his brother.
40. I want you to try all.
41. John won me in tennis.
42. They have banks in their house instead of chairs.
43. Which is Beethoven's latest symphony?
44. He owns about twenty-five acres of ground in Germany.
45. I wait my brother will be here on the fifth.
46. It is not the politic of this store to give cash refunds.
47. Human meat is very fatty.
48. I went to the toilet but it was taken.
49. I wish you wouldn't treat me like a three-year-old.
50. Remember me to mail this letter.

Ejercicio 6

Rellene el espacio en blanco con la traducción de la palabra que aparece entre paréntesis.

1. They give you _____ instead of plates in that restaurant. (fuente)
2. _____ your sister to bring her homework. (recordar)
3. I have _____ Phineas since he was a baby. (conocer)

4. The flight to Seattle is _____ three hours long. (más)

5. It is difficult to live with more than three _____ . (personas)

6. Do you know what eighty-eight _____ nine is? (menos)

7. _____ has shown us that it doesn't work. (historia)

8. How much did you _____ that? (pagar)

9. I _____ he _____ to live in New York. (pensar)

10. She wants me _____ her _____ to swim before the summer. (enseñar)

11. If you don't hurry you are going to _____ the boat. (perder)

12. The _____ was not enough _____ for him to sit down. (sitio)

13. We went bowling but I only _____ . (mirar)

14. It is a good idea to buy life _____ when you are young. (seguro)

15. He should be back in a _____ of hours. (par)

16. _____ is the influence of the public for political motivations. (publicidad)

17. The only _____ I have of my childhood are happy ones. (recuerdo)

18. He could only find a _____ as a waiter. (trabajo)

19. The president must _____ the bill within ten days. (aprobar)

20. They hired private police to _____ their house. (guardar)

21. They don't want to _____ the party just because he can't make it. (suspender)

22. If I were a painter, I would _____ a lot more. (cobrar)

23. Why don't you _____ your sister to come? (invitar)

24. We had only been gone for two days and already she wanted us to _____ . (volver)

25. I have five brothers and sisters and _____ of them look like me. (ninguno)

26. I prefer not to _____ at night. (conducir)

27. I don't think _____ of my two brothers will come. (cualquiera)

28. I hate it when she _____ crying for no reason. (ponerse)

29. Can I help you _____ those bags? (llevar)

30. Don't _____ to call me when you arrive. (dejar)

31. The sales clerk asked the _____ what she wanted. (cliente)

32. Columbus's _____ must have been exciting. (viaje)

33. My _____ has only three burners. (cocina)

34. The library is open to the _____ . (público)

35. He _____ a lot more money now that they gave him a raise. (cobrar)

36. _____ you can see, I have nothing up my sleeve. (como)

37. His chances of winning are almost _____ . (cero)

38. Do you think Alex and Madeline _____ ? (parecer)

39. He had a party and invited the _____ family. (todo)

40. You have to study a lot if you want to _____ a lot of money. (ganar)

41. He went to work one Friday and the boss _____ him. (despedir)

42. What is your favorite _____ of cereal? (marca)

43. He has a(n) _____ on the fith and sixth. (piso)

44. The _____ person in bed should turn off the light. (último)

45. They went on vacation with another _____ . (matrimonio)

46. When it snows in the city, the snow melts as soon as it hits the _____ . (tierra)

47. After removing all the jewels from the safe, he _____ the door. (dirigirse)

48. If you don't _____ a lot, you will not be disappointed. (esperar)

49. Many of those who study law later go into _____ . (política)

50. She doesn't seem to _____ in anything. (creer)

Malas traducciones

A l tratar de hablar en una lengua extranjera es frecuente traducir lo que queremos decir tal como lo diríamos en nuestro propio idioma, palabra por palabra, en lugar de recurrir a las expresiones que son propias de la otra. Recogemos aquí unos ejemplos de este tipo de errores.

AGREE
— *Expresión incorrecta: John is agreed with me on politics.*
— *Expresión correcta:*
John «agrees» with me on politics.
John está de acuerdo conmigo en política.
O:
John and I «agree» on politics.
John y yo estamos de acuerdo en política.

ALWAYS WHEN
— *Expresión incorrecta: Always when he comes home late, he brings her flowers.*

— *Expresión correcta:*
«*Whenever*» *he comes home late, he brings her flowers.*
Siempre que llega tarde a casa, le lleva flores.

ANOTHER TIME
— *Expresión incorrecta: It was so exciting be wanted to do it another time.*
— *Expresión correcta:*
It was so exciting be wanted to do it «again».
Era tan emocionante que quería hacerlo otra vez.

AS
— *Expresión incorrecta: I worked as secretary for three months.*
— *Expresión correcta:*
I worked «as a» secretary for three months.
Trabajé de secretaria tres meses.
«*As a*» *member of the family, I regret those statements.*
Como miembro de la familia, lamento esas declaraciones.
«*As a president*», *it is my duty to inform you of a very sad event.*
Como presidente, es mi deber informarles de un triste suceso.

BORED
— *Expresión incorrecta: The movie was very bored.*
— *Expresión correcta:*

The movie was very «boring».
La película era muy aburrida.

BORING
— *Expresión incorrecta: I was very boring at the party.*
— *Expresión correcta:*
I was very «bored» at the party.
Estaba muy aburrido en la fiesta.

CANDY
— *Expresión incorrecta: The man gave me a candy.*
— *Expresión correcta:*
The man gave me «some candy».
O:
The man gave me «a piece of candy».
El hombre me dio un caramelo.

CAR
— *Expresión incorrecta: Our neighbors don't have car.*
— *Expresión correcta:*
Our neighbors don't have «a car».
Nuestros vecinos no tienen coche.

CARE
— *Expresión incorrecta: Have care!*
— *Expresión correcta:*
«Be careful!»
¡Ten cuidado!

COLD
— *Expresión incorrecta: I have cold.*
— *Expresión correcta:*
«I am cold.»
Tengo frío.
«I have a cold.»
Tengo un resfriado.

DIED
— *Expresión incorrecta: Picasso is died.*
— *Expresión correcta:*
Picasso «is dead».
Picasso ha muerto.

DOCTOR (y todas las demás profesiones)
— *Expresión incorrecta: My father is doctor.*
— *Expresión correcta:*
My father is «a doctor».
Mi padre es médico.

DURING
— *Expresión incorrecta: I was there during two years.*
— *Expresión correcta:*
I was there «for» two years.
Estuve allí durante dos años.

EQUIPMENT
— *Expresión incorrecta: You need a good equipment to scubadive.*
— *Expresión correcta:*

You need «good equipment» to scubadive.
Para hacer submarinismo necesitas un buen equipo.

EVER
— *Expresión incorrecta: She is ever on the telephone.*
— *Expresión correcta:*
She is «always» on the telephone.
Siempre está al teléfono.

FATHER (y otros miembros de la familia)
— *Expresión incorrecta: Mary doesn't have father.*
— *Expresión correcta:*
Mary doesn't «have a father».
Mary no tiene padre.

FEAR
— *Expresión incorrecta: I have fear of dogs.*
— *Expresión correcta:*
«I am afraid of» dogs.
Tengo miedo de los perros.

FEVER
— *Expresión incorrecta: I had fever last night.*
— *Expresión correcta:*
I had «a fever» last night.
Anoche tuve fiebre.

FURNITURE
— *Expresión incorrecta: I bought a new furniture yesterday.*

— *Expresión correcta:*
I bought «a new piece of furniture» yesterday.
Ayer compré un mueble nuevo.

GRAY HAIR
— *Expresión incorrecta: He is tall and has gray hairs.*
— *Expresión correcta:*
He is tall and has «gray hair».
Es alto y tiene canas.

HAIR
— *Expresión incorrecta: She has a beautiful brown hair.*
— *Expresión correcta:*
She has «beautiful brown hair».
Tiene un hermoso cabello castaño.

HAPPEN
— *Expresión incorrecta: What happens you?*
— *Expresión correcta:*
«What's the matter (with you?)»

HEAT
— *Expresión incorrecta: I have heat.*
— *Expresión correcta:*
«I am hot.»
Tengo calor.

HUNGER
— *Expresión incorrecta: I have hunger.*
— *Expresión correcta:*

«*I am hungry.*»
Tengo hambre.

HURRY
— *Expresión incorrecta: I can't wait. I have hurry.*
— *Expresión correcta:*
I can't wait. «*I am in a hurry.*»
No puedo esperar. Tengo prisa.

ICE CREAM
— *Expresión incorrecta: She wants an ice cream.*
— *Expresión correcta:*
She wants «*ice cream*».
Quiere un helado.
Pero:
She wants an ice cream cone.

INFORMATION
— *Expresión incorrecta: If you want a complete information, you must go to the tourist office.*
— *Expresión correcta:*
If you want «*complete information*», *you must go to the tourist office.*
Si desea una información completa, debe ir a la oficina de turismo.

INTEREST
— *Expresión incorrecta: He has always shown interest for music.*
— *Expresión correcta:*

He has always shown «an interest in music».
Siempre ha demostrado interés por la música.

It
— *Expresión incorrecta: Your brother married a princess. I know it.*
— *Expresión correcta:*
Your brother married a princess. «I know».
Tu hermano se casó con una princesa. Lo sé.
Pero:
Do you know the National Anthem? Yes, I know it.
¿Sabes el himno nacional? Sí, lo sé.

Jealousy
— *Expresión incorrecta: He has a lot of jealousy.*
— *Expresión correcta:*
He «is very jealous».
Tiene muchos celos.
Es muy celoso.

Jewelry
— *Expresión incorrecta: My girlfriend bought me a gold jewelry.*
— *Expresión correcta:*
Mi sister bought me «some (a piece of)» gold jewelry.
Mi hermana me compró una joya de oro.

Lightning
— *Expresión incorrecta: Have you ever seen a lightning?*

— *Expresión correcta:*
  Have you ever seen «lightning»?
  ¿Has visto alguna vez un relámpago?

LIKE
— *Expresión incorrecta: I went to a film last night. It liked me.*
— *Expresión correcta:*
  I went to a film last night. «I liked it».
  Anoche fui a ver una película. Me gustó.

— *Expresión incorrecta: Do you like the spinach?*
— *Expresión correcta:*
  Do you like «spinach»?
  ¿Te gustan las espinacas?

— *Expresión incorrecta: Do you like fish? Yes, I like.*
— *Expresión correcta:*
  Do you like fish? Yes, «I like it».
  ¿Te gusta el pescado? Sí, me gusta.

MAKE
— *Expresión incorrecta: I'll make you know when I want to see you again.*
— *Expresión correcta:*
  I'll «let» you know when I want to see you again.
  Te haré saber cuándo quiero verte de nuevo.

— *Expresión incorrecta: He made me a very difficult question.*

— *Expresión correcta:*
He «asked» me a very difficult question.
Me hizo una pregunta muy difícil.

— *Expresión incorrecta: They made me a lot of presents for my birthday.*
— *Expresión correcta:*
They «gave» me a lot of presents for my birthday.
Para mi cumpleaños me hicieron muchos regalos.

MEAN
— *Expresión incorrecta: What means «overwhelm»?*
— *Expresión correcta:*
What does «overwhelm» mean?
¿Qué quiere decir «overwhelm»?

MEMORY
— *Expresión incorrecta: She knows the words to that song by memory.*
— *Expresión correcta:*
She knows the words to that song «by heart».
Sabe la letra de esa canción de memoria.

MERCHANDISE
— *Expresión incorrecta: He exported an illegal merchandise.*
— *Expresión correcta:*
He exported «Illegal merchandise».
Exportó una mercancía ilegal.

MILLION
— *Expresión incorrecta: He has two millions of dollars.*
— *Expresión correcta:*
He has «two million dollars».
Tiene dos millones de dólares.
Pero:
He has millions of dollars.
Tiene millones de dólares.

NEWS
— *Expresión incorrecta: He gave me a good news.*
— *Expresión correcta:*
He gave me «some (a piece of)» good news.
Me dio una buena noticia.

NO
— *Expresión incorrecta: Terry stayed home but Michael no.*
— *Expresión correcta:*
Terry stayed home but Michael and his girlfriend «did not».
Terry se quedó en casa, pero Michael y su novia, no.

— *Expresión incorrecta: I like drinking coffee but no in the evening.*
— *Expresión correcta:*
I like drinking coffee but «not» in the evening.
Me gusta tomar café pero no por la noche.

NONSENSE
— *Expresión incorrecta: He is always saying nonsenses.*
— *Expresión correcta:*
  He is always «talking nonsense».
  Siempre dice tonterías.

NOTHING
— *Expresión incorrecta: He didn't do nothing.*
— *Expresión correcta:*
  He didn't do «anything».
  No hizo nada.
  O:
  He did «nothing».

OF
— *Expresión incorrecta: He was red of embarrassment.*
— *Expresión correcta:*
  He was «red with» embarrassment.
  Estaba rojo de vergüenza.

— *Expresión incorrecta: The reason of his behavior is not clear.*
— *Expresión correcta:*
  The reason for his behavior is not clear.
  La razón de su comportamiento no está clara.

PASS
— *Expresión incorrecta: I passed the weekend in bed.*
— *Expresión correcta:*

I «spent» the weekend in bed.
Pasé el fin de semana en la cama.

— *Expresión incorrecta: What passes you?*
— *Expresión correcta:*
  «*What's the matter with you?*»
  O:
  «*What's wrong*»?
  ¿Qué te pasa?

REASON
— *Expresión incorrecta: He always thinks he has the reason.*
— *Expresión correcta:*
  He always thinks «he is right».
  Siempre cree que tiene razón.

RIGHT
— *Expresión incorrecta: All children have right to a good education.*
— *Expresión correcta:*
  All children have «a (the)» right to a good education.
  Todos los niños tienen derecho a una buena educación.

SILVERWARE
— *Expresión incorrecta: Put the silverwares on the table.*
— *Expresión correcta:*
  Put the «silverware» on the table.
  Pon los cubiertos en la mesa.

SLEEP
— *Expresión incorrecta: I have sleep.*
— *Expresión correcta:*
  «*I am sleepy*».
  Tengo sueño.

— *Expresión incorrecta: He is slept.*
— *Expresión correcta:*
  He is «*asleep*».
  Está dormido.

SOON
— *Expresión incorrecta: I always wake up soon in the morning.*
— *Expresión correcta:*
  I always wake up «*early*» in the morning.
  Siempre me levanto pronto por la mañana.
  Pero:
  I'll see you soon.
  Hasta pronto.

SUCCES
— *Expresión incorrecta: He has success.*
— *Expresión correcta:*
  He «*is successful*».
  Tiene éxito.

THAT
— *Expresión incorrecta: I want that he stay.*
— *Expresión correcta:*

I want «him to stay».
Quiero que se quede.
— *Expresión incorrecta: Remind me that I feed the cat.*
— *Expresión correcta:*
Remind me «to» feed the cat.
Recuérdame que le dé de comer al gato.

— *Expresión incorrecta: He is taller that Tom.*
— *Expresión correcta:*
He is taller «than» Tom.
Es más alto que Tom.

THUNDER
— *Expresión incorrecta: That was a very loud thunder.*
— *Expresión correcta:*
That was «very loud thunder».
Ha sido un trueno muy fuerte.

TIRED
— *Expresión incorrecta: Moving is very tired.*
— *Expresión correcta:*
Moving is very «tiring».
Cambiarse de casa es muy cansado.
Pero:
I was very tired last night.
Anoche estaba muy cansado.

TOAST
— *Expresión incorrecta: Would you like two toasts for breakfast?*

— *Expresión correcta:*
Would you like two « pieces of toast» for break-fast?
¿Quieres dos tostadas para desayunar?

WEATHER

— *Expresión incorrecta: We had a marvelous weather last month.*
— *Expresión correcta:*
We had «marvelous weather» last month.
El mes pasado tuvimos un tiempo maravilloso.

WHITE HAIR

— *Expresión incorrecta: My father had white hair when he was thirty.*
— *Expresión correcta:*
My father and my grandfather had «gray hair» when they were thirty.
Mi padre y mi abuelo tenían el pelo blanco a los treinta años.

YEARS

I have ten years.
— *Expresión correcta:*
«I am ten years old».
O bien:
«I am ten.»
«I am ten years of age».
Tengo diez años.

Ejercicios

Ejercicio 7

Traduzca las frases siguientes al inglés.

1. El niño estaba muy aburrido en el museo.
2. Debes tener mucho cuidado por la noche.
3. El *rock and roll* no está muerto.
4. Viví en Europa diez años.
5. Explicó toda la historia otra vez.
6. Tengo miedo a la oscuridad.
7. Siempre que llegas a casa me encuentras en la cocina.
8. He visto un mueble muy bonito para el comedor.
9. ¿Qué te pasa en la pierna?
10. (Él) Tiene prisa.
11. A la edad de tres años mostró interés por el arte.
12. (Él) Tenía celos porque su madre le hizo un regalo a su hermano.
13. Mi padre siempre me manda un regalo de cumpleaños.
14. No se deben hacer preguntas indiscretas.
15. ¿Qué quiere decir «boardwalk»?
16. Te despertaré temprano.
17. Había millones de pájaros en los árboles.
18. No quería tener nada que ver con ellos.
19. No comprendo la razón de su marcha.
20. ¿Que pasó entre tú y María?
21. Bob tiene razón.

22. Mi madre tiene cubiertos para veinte personas.

23. Mi hermana tiene seis años más que yo.

24. Parece un tiempo de invierno.

25. No me gustan las tostadas con mermelada.

26. ¿No crees que es cansado trabajar con niños?

27. Anoche había truenos y relámpagos.

28. Es más lista de lo que piensas.

29. Quiero que (él) vaya a la tienda a comprar leche.

30. No tiene mucho éxito pero es feliz.

31. El niño tiene mucho sueño.

32. (Él) Tiene derecho a saber lo que hacen con su dinero.

33. Léemelo pero no tan deprisa.

34. Te traigo una buena noticia.

35. A mí me gusta.

36. Ayer probé el hígado y me gustó.

37. Lleva unas joyas muy llamativas.

38. Termina eso que son casi las siete. Ya lo sé. Ahora voy.

39. La policía ha recibido una información por télex.

40. Si tienes hambre, hay comida en la nevera.

41. Si tienes calor, abre la ventana.

42. Tiene el pelo muy largo.

43. Mi padre no tiene canas.

44. Mañana tienes que despertarte muy temprano para coger el autobús.

45. Cuando tengas fiebre, tómate una aspirina.

46. No está casado pero tiene suegra.

47. Quiere estar siempre con ella.

48. Cuando sea mayor quiero ser maestro.

49. Hace calor pero tengo frío.
50. Me parece que he cogido un resfriado.

Ejercicio 8

Corrija las siguientes frases si hace falta.

1. If you don't have care, you will break it.
2. I have license but I don't have car.
3. If you do it another time, I'll spank you.
4. They make 3 millions of dollars a year.
5. I'd like to stay but I'm in a hurry.
6. I don't think you have a right to say that.
7. He made me a question I couldn't answer.
8. She doesn't want a chocolate ice cream.
9. What happens when you mix oil and water?
10. He was green of envy.
11. She doesn't have as many years as I do.
12. If he didn't have as much jealousy, she'd love him more.
13. My father is doctor and my brothers are doctors too.
14. I don't like eating with cheap silverwares.
15. Never accept candies from a stranger.
16. I have fear of to no pass the exam.
17. Everyone is slept but I don't feel sleeping.
18. Have you ever worked as waiter?
19. He likes chicken but no turkey.
20. The party was so bored everyone left soon.

21. I don't know if I want that you do that.
22. Always when it's windy, that window breaks.
23. Do you always have such a bad weather in August?
24. I always catch a cold when I work in that room.
25. The man who dead last week was very wealthy.
26. If he has the reason, we're in trouble.
27. He has had fever for three days.
28. Do you know what freedom means?
29. I am really hunger.
30. He is not agreed with my way of thinking.
31. I would like to get a new furniture for the bedroom.
32. If you go to a bored movie you are boring.
33. He didn't see his mother during ten years.
34. They are ever arguing.
35. Men with white hair are interesting.
36. That was a very important information he gave us.
37. He has always had interest for music.
38. Does anybody have Mark's telephone number? I know it by heart.
39. I have fear when I walk down dark alleys alone.
40. No news is a good news.
41. I don't know why he didn't do nothing when they robbed his house.
42. You should pass a few days at my house in the mountains.
43. He had a big success after his last movie.
44. John has never had father.
45. I'll make you know when the dress is ready.

46. She has the hair down to her waist.
47. Did you see E.T.? Yes, and I liked.
48. I never have heat.
49. If you don't like this, you can return it.
50. I don't have to put up with those nonsenses.

Ejercicio 9

Rellene los espacios en blanco con la(s) palabra(s) apropiada(s).

1. _____ he comes to town, he brings the children a gift.
   (Always when / Always / Ever / Whenever)
2. The party was so _____ everyone left early.
   (bored / boring / bore / bores)
3. John doesn't have _____ .
   (car / cars any / any car / a car)
4. My father has been _____ for ten years.
   (die / died / dead / death)
5. She always has _____ .
   (fever / a fever / some fevers / any fevers)
6. _____ ? Nothing, really. I'm just tired.
   (What happens you? / What happens to you? / What matters you? / What's the matter with you?)
7. He wanted _____ about tomorrow night's game.
   (informations / some informations / an information / information)

8. My son _____ ten years old.
   (has / have / is / will have)
9. His sister is taller _____ he is.
   (then / that / than / Ø)
10. I prefer driving _____ in the morning to late at night.
    (soon / early / plenty / prone)
11. You have _____ right to remain silent.
    (the / to / your / Ø)
12. There isn't _____ we can do now.
    (nothing / anything / something / that)
13. We heard _____ on the radio.
    (a good news / some good news / a good new / some good new)
14. _____
    (What mean book? / What does mean book? / What book means? / What does book mean?
15. I go to the opera a lot. _____
    (It likes me. / Me likes it. / I like me. / I like it.)
16. Feel free to _____ me as many questions as you want.
    (do / make / question / ask)
17. I always buy my girlfriend _____ gold jewelry for her birthday.
    (a / one / any / some)
18. _____
    (His wife is very jealous. / His wife is a lot jealous. / His wife has a lot of jealousies. / His wife has very jealousies.)

19. Tim has shown _____ history ever since he was very young.

(interest for / an interest for / an interest in / to interest in)

20. _____

(She wants ice cream cone. / She wants an ice cream cone. / She wants a cone of ice cream. / She wants an ice cream.)

21. The little boy wanted to ride on his father's shoulders _____ .

(one time more / another time / again / another)

22. She has worked _____ nurse since she was twenty one.

(as / as a / like / like a)

23. Everyone in the movie theater was so _____ that they were all yawning.

(bored / boring / bores / bore)

24. My mother told me not to accept _____ from strangers.

(a candy / some candies / candy / candies)

25. You should _____ when you drive at night.

(have extra care / be extra care / have extra careful / be extra careful)

26. I have a runny nose and a headache. I think _____ .

(I am a cold / I have a cold / I am cold / I have cold)

27. When I grow up, I want to be _____ .

(lawyer / a lawyer / one lawyer / lawyers)

28. I have been in this city _____ five years.
(for / since / ever since / during)

29. Martha has _____ brother-in-law in each country.
(some / no / a / Ø)

30. My sister passed the exam but I _____ .
(didn't / not / don't / no)

31. This is not _____ for sailing.
(a weather ideal / an ideal weather / ideal weather / weather ideal)

32. I always have _____ for breakfast.
(two toast / two pieces of toasts / two toasts / two pieces of toast)

33. Working as a mailman must be very _____ .
(tired / tiring / tire / tires)

34. The reason why he _____ is that he is sincere.
(has so much success / is so much success / has so successful / is so successful)

35. I couldn't talk to him because when I called he _____ .
(had sleep / was sleepy / had slept / was asleep)

36. You can't discuss anything with him because he always thinks he _____ .
(has the right / is reason / has the reason / is right)

37. You don't understand him because he is constantly _____ .
(saying nonsense / saying nonsenses / talking nonsense / talking nonsenses)

38. I like sugar in my coffee but _____ .

(in my tea not / no in my tea / in my tea no / not in my tea)

39. David made _____ in one transaction.

(two million dollars / two millions dollars / two millions of dollars / two million of dollars)

40. Small children always _____ indiscreet questions.

(make / question / ask / do)

41. The company will _____ you know if you get the job.

(make / have / to let / let)

42. Almost all kids like _____ .

(very liver / one liver / the liver / liver)

43. A: Your mother is not feeling well.

B: _____ . I saw her this morning.

(I know / I know it / I knew it / I know)

44. I can't do that right now because I _____ .

(have a hurry / am in hurry / have hurry / am in a hurry)

45. My sister has _____ .

(a short curly hair / short curly hair / the hair short and curly / the short curly hair)

46. They bought _____ that is too big for their living room.

(furnitures / a piece of furniture / a furniture / some furnitures)

47. John never does _____ to help around the house.

(anything / something / everything / nothing)
48. Bob _____ plays basketball on Sundays.

(ever / forever / always / again)
49. If you want to play hockey, you have to buy

_____ .

(an expensive equipment / expensive equipment / some expensive equipments / expensive equipments)
50. Arthur and I _____ on anything.

(are not of agree / do not agreed / are not agree / do not agree)

Verbos seguidos de diferente preposición en inglés y en español

Los conocidos *phrasal verbs* son aquellos que van acompañados de una preposición. En muchos casos no existe una correspondencia entre el inglés y el español.

Esto significa que podemos encontrarnos con algunos verbos que van seguidos de una preposición distinta en cada una de las lenguas, y otros verbos que van acompañados de preposición en una lengua mientras que en la otra no.

En este apartado encontrará una relación de todos ellos.

APPLY FOR = SOLICITAR
> *He applied for a civil servant's position.*
> Solicitó un puesto de funcionario.

APPROVE OF = APROBAR
> *He doesn't approve of sex and violence in films.*
> No aprueba ni el sexo ni la violencia en las películas.

ARRIVE AT = LLEGAR A *(a building, a park, conclusion)*
>He arrived at the airport at seven o'clock.
>Llegó al aeropuerto a las siete.

ARRIVE IN = LLEGAR A *(a city, state or country)*
>*He arrived in Madrid before I did.*
>Llegó a Madrid antes que yo.

ASK ABOUT = PREGUNTAR POR
>*When I saw James and Margaret, they asked about you.*
>Cuando vi a James y a Margaret preguntaron por ti.

ASK FOR = PEDIR
>*The child asked for a glass of water.*
>El niño pidió un vaso de agua.

ATTEND = ESTAR PRESENTE EN, ASISTIR A
>*He attended the meeting in his pajamas.*
>Asistió a la reunión en pijama.

BE BAD AT = SER MALO
>*I'm very bad at telling jokes.*
>Soy muy malo contando chistes.

BE CRUEL TO = SER CRUEL CON
>*Ferdinand is always cruel to his sister.*
>Ferdinand siempre es cruel con su hermana.

BE (DRESSED) IN = IR (VESTIDO) DE
I was talking to the woman (dressed) in red.
Estaba hablando con la mujer (vestida) de rojo.

BE ENGAGED TO = ESTAR PROMETIDO A/CON
Mary is engaged to John.
Mary está prometida a/con John.

BE FED UP WITH = ESTAR HARTO DE
He was fed up with his incompetent assistants.
Estaba harto de sus incompetentes ayudantes.

BE ILL WITH = ESTAR ENFERMO DE
The teacher is ill with hepatitis.
El maestro está enfermo de hepatitis.

BE INDEBTED TO = ESTAR EN DEUDA CON
I'm eternally indebted to all of my teachers.
Estaré eternamente en deuda con todos mis profesores.

BE IN LOVE WITH = ESTAR ENAMORADO DE
Phillip is in love with Greta Garbo.
Phillip está enamorado de Greta Garbo.

BE KIND TO = SER AMABLE CON
You should be kind to your grandparents.
Debes ser amable con tus abuelos.

BE LUCKY AT *(games, gambling)* = TENER SUERTE EN
He is lucky at games.
Tiene suerte en el juego.

BE MAD *(angry)* AT = ESTAR ENFADADO CON
Walter is mad at his cousin.
Walter está enfadado con su primo.

BE MARRIED TO = ESTAR CASADO CON
Fred is married to Elissabeth, John's sister.
Fred está casado con Elissabeth, la hermana de
John.

BE NAMED AFTER = LLEVAR EL NOMBRE DE
He is named after his uncle.
Lleva el nombre de su tío.

BE NEAR = ESTAR CERCA DE
Our house is near the river.
Nuestra casa está cerca del río.

BE NEXT TO = ESTAR AL LADO DE
The house that is next to ours is pink.
La casa que está al lado de la nuestra es de color
rosa.

BE NICE TO = SER AMABLE CON
David is nice to his students.
David es amable con sus alumnos.

BE POLITE TO = SER CORTÉS CON
He is the only student in the class who is polite to the teacher.
Es el único alumno de la clase que es cortés con el profesor.

BE RELATED TO = SER PARIENTE DE, ESTAR EMPARENTADO CON
We are distantly related to the King.
Somos parientes lejanos del Rey.

BE RELATED TO = ESTAR RELACIONADO CON
His view of the facts is hardly related to reality.
Su visión de los hechos apenas está relacionada con la realidad.

BE RUDE TO = SER DESCORTÉS CON
Small children should be taught not to be rude to their elders.
Hay que enseñar a los niños pequeños a no ser descorteses con los mayores.

BE SATISFIED WITH = ESTAR SATISFECHO DE/CON
The actor was very satisfied with his performance.
El actor estaba muy satisfecho de su actuación.

BE SURROUNDED BY = ESTAR RODEADO DE
We were surrounded by water.
Estábamos rodeados de agua.

BET ON = APOSTAR POR
> *He always bets on the home team.*
> Siempre apuesta por el equipo de casa.

COMMENT ON = COMENTAR
> *They commented on his rudeness.*
> Comentaron su mala educación.

CONCEAL FROM = OCULTAR A
> *He concealed his watch from the robbers.*
> Ocultó el reloj a los ladrones.

CONGRATULATE ON = FELICITAR POR
> *The director congratulated the actress on her performance.*
> El director felicitó a la actriz por su actuación.

CONSIST OF = CONSISTIR EN *(componerse de)*
> *The San Francisco Bay Area consists of nine counties.*
> El área de la bahía de San Francisco consiste en nueve condados.

CONTRIBUTE = CONTRIBUIR CON
> *He contributed 400 dollars to the fund.*
> Contribuyó al fondo con 400 dólares.

COUNT ON/UPON = CONTAR CON
> *You can count on my help.*
> Puedes contar con mi ayuda.

COVER WITH = CUBRIR DE
The mountain was covered with snow.
El monte estaba cubierto de nieve.

DECIDE ON = DECIDIRSE POR
After discussing it a lot, we decided on black.
Después de hablarlo mucho, nos decidimos por el negro.

DELIGHT IN = DELEITARSE CON/EN
He delighted in the applause of the audience.
Se deleitaba con/en el aplauso del público.

DEPEND ON = DEPENDER DE
Everything depends on you.
Todo depende de ti.

DISCRIMINATE AGAINST = DISCRIMINAR A
Discriminating against women is strongly punishable by law.
Discriminar a las mujeres está duramente castigado por la ley.

DIVORCE = DIVORCIARSE DE
Helen finally divorced her husband.
Helen se divorció por fin de su marido.

DREAM OF/ABOUT = SOÑAR CON
I dreamed of a tall blond man.
Soñé con un hombre alto y rubio.

FALL IN LOVE WITH = ENAMORARSE DE
He fell in love with her the first time he saw her.
Se enamoró de ella la primera vez que la vio.

FEED ON = ALIMENTARSE DE
Whales feed on small fish.
Las ballenas se alimentan de peces pequeños.

FILL WITH = LLENAR DE
Fill up the tank with super, please.
Llene el depósito de súper, por favor.

HAVE PERMISSION TO = TENER PERMISO PARA
He doesn't have permission to leave the table.
No tiene permiso para levantarse de la mesa.

HURT = HACER DAÑO A; HACERSE DAÑO EN
I don't like hurting people.
No me gusta hacerle daño a la gente.

He hurt his leg.
Se hizo daño en la pierna.

KNOW HOW TO = SABER
Does he know how to ride a bike?
¿Sabe ir en bicicleta?

LAUGH AT = REÍRSE DE
Teachers often laugh at their students' mistakes.
Los profesores se ríen muchas veces de las equivocaciones de sus alumnos.

LEARN HOW TO = APRENDER A
I am learning how to sew.
Estoy aprendiendo a coser.

LISTEN TO = ESCUCHAR
He listens to the radio all the time.
Escucha constantemente la radio.

LIVE BY = VIVIR DE
He lives by working in the fields.
Vive de trabajar en el campo.

LIVE ON = VIVIR DE *(alimentarse de)*
He lives on bread and water.
Vive de pan y agua.

He lives on the interest from his capital.
Vive de los intereses de su capital.

MARVEL AT = MARAVILLARSE DE
He marvelled at the height of the tower.
Se maravilló de la altura de la torre.

OPERATE ON = FUNCIONAR CON
The new toy operates on batteries.
El juguete nuevo funciona con pilas.

PAY FOR = PAGAR
I paid for his coffee.
Le pagué el café.

PLEAD WITH = SUPLICAR A
The murderer's mother pleaded with the judge.
La madre del asesino le suplicó al juez.

PROVIDE WITH = PROPORCIONAR
His father provided him with everything he needed to succeed.
Su padre le proporcionó todo lo que necesitaba para tener éxito.

REMIND OF = RECORDAR A
That man reminds me of my father.
Ese hombre me recuerda a mi padre.

RESULT IN = RESULTAR, DAR LUGAR A
The argument resulted in the imprisonment of both of them.
De la discusión resultó el encarcelamiento de ambos.

STAY AT = ALOJARSE EN
We stayed at a beautiful hotel.
Nos alojamos en un bonito hotel.

STEAL FROM = ROBAR A
He stole a book from his roommate.
Le robó un libro a su compañero de cuarto.

STOP AT = PARAR EN/ANTE
He is very ambitious; he doesn't stop at anything.
Es muy ambicioso, no se detiene ante nada.

STUDY UNDER = ESTUDIAR CON
He studied philosophy under Sartre.
Estudió filosofía con Sartre.

SUPPLY WITH = SUMINISTRAR
The company that used to supply us with paper closed down.
La empresa que nos suministraba papel ha cerrado.

TALK ABOUT = HABLAR DE
He always talks about starting his own business.
Siempre habla de abrir un negocio propio.

TASTE OF = SABER A
This pastry tastes of cognac.
Este pastel sabe a coñac.

TEACH HOW TO = ENSEÑAR A
He taught the boys how to swim.
Enseñó a los chicos a nadar.

THINK OF = PENSAR EN
He is always thinking of ways to please her.
Siempre está pensando en maneras de complacerla.

TRUST IN = CONFIAR EN, FIARSE DE
He trusts in my ability to convince her.
Se fía de mi habilidad para convencerla.

TRUST WITH = CONFIAR
I'd trust him with my life.
Le confiaría mi vida.

VOTE FOR = VOTAR A
He voted for the republican candidate.
Votó al candidato republicano.

WAIT FOR = ESPERAR A
I'll wait for Diana downstairs.
Esperaré a Diana abajo.

WONDER ABOUT = PREGUNTARSE POR
He wondered about her whereabouts.
Se preguntaba por su paradero.

WONDER AT = MARAVILLARSE DE
I wonder at his audacity.
Me maravillo de su audacia.

Ejercicios

Ejercicio 10

Traduzca las frases siguientes al inglés.

1. La equivocación dio lugar a tres muertos y varios heridos.
2. Lo único que le proporcionaba era cariño.

3. Compró una radio que funciona con pilas.

4. Después de haber estudiado con los maestros más renombrados del mundo dejó el piano.

5. Vive del trabajo que hace para su hermana.

6. (Ella) Se rió de todos sus (de él) chistes.

7. Lo conozco hace mucho tiempo y me fío de él.

8. Sólo es amable con la gente que le puede ayudar.

9. Me maravillo de su habilidad con la pelota.

10. (Él) Se hizo daño en la pierna en el accidente.

11. La camarera era descortés con todos los clientes.

12. David está casado con la chica más rica del pueblo.

13. Esos dos acontecimientos no están relacionados con el crimen.

14. Se divorció de ella cuando supo lo que hacía.

15. La policía era muy cortés con los manifestantes.

16. No tienes que pagar el billete hasta que llegues.

17. Estaba harto de sus vecinos y se cambió de casa.

18. (Él) Enseñó a su perro a hacer muchos trucos.

19. Nunca ha estado prometida con nadie.

20. Me gustaría aprender a tocar el piano.

21. Si nos vamos o no, depende del tiempo.

22. ¿Sabes ir a casa solo?

23. (Ella) Se deleita en el agua fría.

24. Lleva el nombre del primer presidente.

25. Nos decidimos por una iglesia pequeña del barrio antiguo de la ciudad.

26. (Él) Es capaz de robarle caramelos a un niño pequeño.

27. No puedes contar con que haga buen tiempo.

28. He estado enamorado de ti desde el primer momento en que te vi.

29. Me enamoré de la hermana de la novia de mi hermano.

30. El político no quería comentar la derrota de su partido.

31. Mary está al lado de la chica de rosa.

32. En la quinta apostó por un caballo blanco.

33. Mi casa está cerca del trabajo.

34. Asistió él al baile sólo porque ella quería.

35. El queso estaba cubierto de hongos verdes.

36. Está enfadado con su hermana porque no ha venido.

37. Soñó con ser el mejor jugador de su equipo.

38. Gonzalo no es cruel con nadie.

39. (Ella) Siempre se viste de negro.

40. Está enfermo de tuberculosis.

41. (Él) Está en deuda con todos sus amigos.

42. (Él) Llenó el vaso de agua y se lo bebió.

43. Los buitres se alimentan de los restos de otros animales.

44. (Él) Ocultó su vida privada a sus compañeros de trabajo.

45. Nos suministraron todo lo que nos hacía falta para escalar la montaña.

46. Siempre habla de cosas que no entiende.

47. Acabo de pensar una actividad maravillosa para la clase.

48. Tienes que llegar al aeropuerto dos horas antes de que salga el vuelo.

49. Llegó a Nueva York el día que nos marchábamos.
50. No creo que la subida de la bolsa esté relacionada con las elecciones.

Ejercicio 11

Corrija las siguientes frases si hace falta.

1. He only talks about cars and money.
2. Mark taught his daughters swimming.
3. We are thinking in going to Italy this year.
4. Discriminating to people can be punished by law.
5. It's easy to be fed up on thirty-five-year-old children.
6. You only need to provide your children food, shelter and affection.
7. The house was surrounded in trees.
8. His international acclaim resulted to his winning the Nobel Prize.
9. The Pope approved the cardinal's attitudes and actions concerning the conflict.
10. The President's plane arrived to the airport at six o'clock.
11. He paid dinner and she bought the drinks afterwards.
12. The rise in prices is not related with the measures taken by the government.
13. It's easy to hurt to people just by talking.

14. I am the worst in tennis in my class.

15. Be nice with your friends.

16. He wants to apply for a job at a large department store.

17. Sometimes I wonder for his true intentions.

18. I don't attend at the faculty meetings if I don't have to.

19. We have a giant pine tree next to our house.

20. The floor was covered of blood.

21. Nobody ever comments his sordid past.

22. Phillip is mad with the whole family.

23. It's just as easy to fall in love of a rich girl.

24. I dreamed with you last night.

25. I always bet for the underdog.

26. He pleaded to his boss to give him the day off.

27. A city's capability to organize the Olympics depends of public support of the idea.

28. If you are cruel with others, they are sure to be cruel with you.

29. You can't count with him to be there on time.

30. Being in love with someone is a marvellous feeling.

31. She is very attractive when she is dressed with green.

32. Have you ever stolen anything to anyone?

33. Concealing your feelings from everyone doesn't help you solve your problems.

34. I don't trust in him enough to leave him alone.

35. I don't like to go there because it reminds me to a bad experience.

36. Everyone laughed her joke.
37. I've been ill of a cold for a month.
38. Arnold is married with Marvin's sister.
39. My boss congratulated me for a job well done.
40. There is a pharmacy near to my house.
41. He was very rude with us when we came in.
42. They don't have permission to use his songs.
43. Deciding for the right school is not easy.
44. I was indebted with my parents after they helped me through college.
45. He carries the name of his father.
46. She was filled of excitement after winning the prize.
47. Mr. Sadin delighted with the pain of his guests.
48. Birds feed in worms and insects.
49. He doesn't know to swim.
50. He hurt on his head when he walked through the doorway.

Ejercicio 12

Rellene los espacios en blanco con la preposición apropiada, si es necesario.

1. He concealed his previous-marriage _____ her.
2. You remind me _____ a girlfriend I once had.
3. He stole money _____ all his friends.
4. You shouldn't laugh _____ small children when they do something impolite.

5. Have you seen «The Woman _____ Red»?

6. He is always ill _____ something:

7. He was married _____ a very nice girl for a while.

8. He was counting _____ the money he had left with her.

9. We congratulated the other team _____ their victory.

10. He falls in love _____ a new girl every year.

11. They filled the bowl _____ soup.

12. Adrienne never gets mad _____ anyone.

13. I have never seen anyone delight _____ eating as much as Stephen.

14. I didn't want to comment _____ what she said about my sister.

15. The seals in the zoo feed _____ live fish.

16. Brigitte's face was covered _____ make-up.

17. Phineas is bad _____ chess.

18. The beggar asked the passer-by to have pity _____ him.

19. Paul hurt _____ his chin when he fell down.

20. I can't wait _____ you much longer.

21. Lenny Beatty is not related _____ Warren.

22. I don't think he could live _____ a vegetarian diet.

23. We were surrounded _____ foreigners at the beach.

24. It's easy to be polite _____ people.

25. Her father provided her _____ a good education.

26. George always asks _____ more than he needs.

27. She was fed up _____ having the same thing for breakfast every morning.

28. She divorced _____ her husband when she found out.

29. He never talks _____ what happened to him in the war.

30. Mark was engaged _____ a woman from Rome.

31. She is listening _____ a very old song.

32. He thought _____ a very safe way to send the wine.

33. The bus driver was very rude _____ the passengers.

34. Some large firms discriminate _____ married women.

35. The teacher was not satisfied _____ the results of his student's exams.

36. The riot resulted _____ twelve arrests and numerous injuries.

37. His radio operates _____ 220 V current.

38. Your mother would never approve _____ that kind of behavior.

39. They stayed _____ a hotel because we had no room.

40. Whenever Sarah arrives _____ San Francisco, she gets nostalgic.

41. Carlos studied art _____ his grandfather, who is a well known artist.

42. I'll pay _____ lunch if you pay _____ the taxi

home.

43. Maria was very nice _____ Stephen and Terry while they were here.

44. The school supplies the students _____ paper, but they must bring their own _____ pens and pencils.

45. Nicole applied _____ a job with the Public Defender's Office.

46. I am luckier _____ cards than _____ roulette.

47. John has to leave at six to attend _____ a meeting.

48. I don't like to depend _____ people to get me to work on time.

49. His stereo is next _____ his television.

50. We'd better stop _____ the first sign of disapproval.

SOLUCIONARIO

Términos engañosos: ejercicios

Ejercicio 1

1. Robert siempre ayuda a su madre en las tareas domésticas.
2. Después de registrarnos en recepción, el mozo nos subió el equipaje.
3. Quiero que os calléis todos.
4. Si al principio no tienes éxito, inténtalo otra vez.
5. La travesía de Brindisi a Corfú fue muy agitada.
6. Terry es bastante locuaz y no sabe escuchar.
7. No puedo grabar aquella canción.
8. La bomba estalló y mató a tres policías.
9. En realidad, me da igual que vengas o no.
10. Es un firme partidario de los ideales del comunismo.
11. Retiraron todos esos productos del mercado.
12. Tiene una manera especial de tratar a la gente.
13. La mejor parte de la obra era la discusión entre los dos protagonistas.
14. Hubo muchas bajas durante la guerra.

15. Peter fue a un congreso de directores de escuelas de idiomas.

16. El cobrador nos pidió los billetes, pero los habíamos perdido.

17. Nos dieron instrucciones para llegar a la casa que tienen en el campo.

18. No me gusta beber café en taza.

19. Llevó un sombrero muy llamativo a la boda.

20. Trabajó como redactor en el periódico local durante veinticinco años.

21. Buscaba la salida pero no la encontraba.

22. Hay un jarrón en la mesa.

23. Ted es un anfitrión muy gentil.

24. Fran quedó consternada cuando pedí la mano de Mary.

25. Al estaba avergonzado cuando llegué a la ciudad.

26. Me gusta la tela que usaron para hacer ese vestido.

27. El director no cree que aquel joven pueda mejorar.

28. De chico era conocido por su ingenio.

29. Había un aviso diciendo que el lunes no habría clase.

30. Fui a la biblioteca a buscar un libro.

31. Se le ocurrió una idea original.

32. Hizo una afirmación extremadamente difamatoria sobre su madre.

33. Daniel es un médico excelente.

34. Brian estaba ocupadísimo con su hijo recién nacido.

35. El maestro pidió a los alumnos que repitieran el estribillo.
36. He oído muchas habladurías por la escuela.
37. Ringo era la persona más cuerda de nuestra familia.
38. Es un verdadero erudito.
39. Su hermano le aconsejó dónde ir a la universidad.
40. Me siento despreciado desde la fiesta de anoche.
41. Posee un ejemplar muy raro de Ulises.
42. Aquella palabra tiene varias acepciones.
43. El presidente se refirió a la crisis de Centroamérica.
44. Su secretaria le dijo lo que había en el orden del día.
45. Oscilaba entre la alta sociedad y la pobreza.
46. El locutor dijo que el producto estaría pronto en el mercado.
47. Necesito un ayudante en el trabajo.
48. Cuando éramos jóvenes solíamos jugar en la buhardilla.
49. Después de cenar volvió al cuartel.
50. Es una persona muy franca.

Ejercicio 2

1. He is a very sensitive boy.
2. The building can house eight hundred students.

3. You must stir it up well before using it.

4. We have to summarize the novel.

5. I recommend it to you because it is a reliable school.

6. He passed the exam without studying.

7. The doctor asked him to breathe in.

8. She got excellent grades this year.

9. 1 warned you that it would rain.

10. The lawyer left the court furious.

11. They awarded him the house.

12. The powers have agreed upon meeting.

13. My Spanish teacher is very nice.

14. An adolescent's social life is as important as his studies.

15. Ours is an era of inconstant politicians.

16. Monks make a vow of poverty.

17. The boss wanted a list of the employees involved.

18. The doctor examined all those affected.

19. They advertised a new powder that gets out stains without wetting the fabric.

20. The inauguration of the sixth International Jazz Festival of San Francisco was a success.

21. I am certain it's a trap.

22. He has a tendency to use commonplaces.

23. They threw him out of the company for being lazy and arriving late.

24. The firemen extinguished the fire just in time.

25. As a child she was skinny.

26. My grandmother always kept a picture of the Virgin under her pillow.

27. The new head of the Health Department is a woman.
28. Stephen was so noisy that they asked him to leave the bar.
29. Madeleine has a bad temper.
30. Your relatives can not testify on your behalf.
31. I had never experienced such a strange thing.
32. I think your friend's husband is reliable.
33. The children were very excited when they left school.
34. Excuse me for being late but a friend kept me.
35. There are many cultivated people who lack good manners.
36. His life is full of misfortune.
37. Actors often sue magazines for not respecting their privacy.
38. It's a fairly ordinary subject.
39. Alfred has had a bad temper ever since he was a boy.
40. Maybe you don't like him, but he is consistent.
41. Laureen was one of the most understanding teachers I had.
42. If you are too complaisant, people will pull your leg.
43. We got on the first class car by mistake.
44. We go to the country every Sunday.
45. She finished high school at sixteen.
46. Comfort is the most important thing on a train.
47. The dragons were made of cardboard.
48. Coal is used a lot in Great Britain.

49. The father liked putting the children to bed.
50. It's very difficult to translate jokes.

Ejercicio 3

1. popularize
2. foreigner
3. coincidence
4. cardboard
5. premises were
6. actors
7. visitor
8. title
9. variety
10. news
11. followers
12. Beavers
13. cartoons
14. charlatan
15. confidants
16. plot
17. beneficial
18. bedrooms
19. barefaced
20. temporary
21. demands
22. record
23. widespread
24. aggravating

25. flowery
26. exhibition
27. raincoat
28. tip
29. humane
30. try
31. sit up
32. indiscreet
33. invested
34. envious
35. library
36. grades
37. newspaper
38. politician
39. sealed
40. beautiful
41. boasted
42. leaflets
43. taste
44. resort
45. outstanding
46. outline
47. endure
48. meeting
49. suspects
50. failed

Términos con correspondencias múltiples: ejercicios

Ejercicio 4

1. I remember when you were young and happy.
2. You have to live in a country to get to know it well.
3. He is more intelligent than he seems.
4. She is a very good person.
5. The elderly have less patience.
6. Has he ever told you the story of how he became famous?
7. Have you paid the phone bill?
8. If you think before you act (acting), you will make fewer mistakes.
9. He teaches mathematics to six-year-olds.
10. He learned Spanish when he was twelve.
11. I lost your book.
12. I'll save your place.
13. The doctor looked at my toe.
14. I'm not sure whether he wants to come or not.
15. I need a pair of leather gloves.

16. Advertising on television is very expensive.
17. They have thousands of souvenir shops in Rome.
18. I can't wear a watch while I work.
19. He wants a job on a newspaper.
20. I don't approve of your sister's behavior.
21. They called the trial off due to the absence of one of the attorneys.
22. You should cash those traveler's checks as soon as you get back.
23. You are invited to a lunch with the Governor.
24. The policeman told the child that he should return (go back) home.
25. Neither of the two roads led to the south.
26. Either of those hats will suit you.
27. She puts perfume on every day.
28. My father let me go to the movies with Pablo and David.
29. He stopped smoking four years ago.
30. He is an architect with very special clients.
31. We took a trip to Venice to attend the film festival.
32. They have an enormous kitchen.
33. The public will not understand his reason.
34. I am one of this bookstore's most regular customers.
35. The king is like any other person.
36. What is the king like?
37. The Hindus invented the zero.
38. You seem (look) bored.
39. I had to work all (the whole) weekend.

40. He earns (makes) a lot more money than me (I do).

41. I don't like saying good-bye.

42. In this neighborhood they judge you by the make of your car.

43. We have an apartment on the coast.

44. I was the last one to see him.

45. I don't believe in marriage.

46. The extraterrestrials didn't want to come down to the Earth.

47. The Pope addressed the people in six languages.

48. I hope it doesn't rain tomorrow.

49. Politics is one of the most privileged professions.

50. I think you are making a mistake (you are wrong).

Ejercicio 5

1. They own a very expensive car. I don't know what make.

2. The source of a river is where it begins.

3. We walked along the promenade for hours.

4. He left the country to get a visa.

5. I spent three weeks with him.

6. You have to do more than attend class.

7. He told me he would come at seven.

8. He speaks French like a native.

9. She choked on her sandwich.

10. My mother always makes us cakes for our birthday.
11. He has experienced the most terrible pain you can imagine.
12. The man with the beard, the black hat and the long coat stole my wallet.
13. We couldn't find any shade on the beach.
14. You should get going soon if you want to catch the train that leaves in half an hour.
15. I met him when I was ten.
16. You remind me of a teacher I had in grammar school.
17. Twelve plus ten equals twenty-two.
18. People are very strange.
19. The fewer brothers and sisters you have the more presents you get.
20. He paid for the dress with his own money.
21. He intended to leave at eight o'clock.
22. You missed your mother.   She left a moment ago.
23. We don't have enough room for a table in the kitchen.
24. I watch TV three hours a day.
25. It isn't a very safe neighborhood.
26. I only have a couple of dollars.
27. We bought a clock to hang on the wall in the kitchen.
28. He has passed all of his exams this year.
29. He failed all of his exams last year.
30. None of my three sisters is married.

31. On a basketball team any player can take the ball out.

32. She always wears very strange hats.

33. He lent me twenty-five dollars until the end of the month.

34. When we were in Macy's ninety per cent of the customers were over eighty years old.

35. The journey (trip) from New York to San Francisco takes fifty-eight hours.

36. Do you have a gas or electric stove?

37. I like going to concerts just to look at the audience.

38. As a tax-payer, I have the right to know what the money is spent on.

39. He doesn't really look like his brother.

40. I want you to try everything.

41. John beat me in tennis.

42. They have benches in their house instead of chairs.

43. Which is Beethoven's last symphony?

44. He owns about twenty-five acres of land in Germany.

45. I hope (expect) my brother will be here on the fifth.

46. It is not the policy of this store to give cash refunds.

47. Human flesh is very fatty.

48. I went to the toilet but it was occupied.

49. Correct.

50. Remind me to mail this letter.

Ejercicio 6

1. platters
2. Remind
3. known
4. over/more than
5. people
6. minus
7. History
8. pay for
9. think-intends
10. to teach-how
11. miss
12. room
13. watched
14. insurance
15. couple
16. Propaganda
17. memories
18. job
19. approve
20. guard
21. call off
22. charge/make/earn
23. ask/invite
24. return/go back
25. none
26. drive
27. either
28. starts

29. carry
30. fail
31. customer
32. voyage(s)
33. stove
34. public
35. makes
36. As
37. nil/zero
38. look alike
39. whole
40. earn/make
41. fired
42. brand
43. apartment-floor
44. last
45. married couple
46. ground
47. headed for
48. expect
49. politics
50. believe

Malas traducciones: ejercicios

Ejercicio 7

1. The child (boy) was very bored at the museum.
2. You should be very careful at night.
3. Rock and roll is not dead.
4. I lived in Europe for ten years.
5. She explained the whole story again.
6. I am afraid of the dark.
7. Whenever you get (arrive) home, you find me in the kitchen.
8. I saw a very nice piece of furniture for the dining room.
9. What's the matter (What's wrong) with your leg?
10. He is in a hurry.
11. At the age of three (at three), he showed an interest in art.
12. He was jealous because his mother gave his brother a present.
13. My father always sends me a birthday present (gift).

14. You (One) shouldn't ask indiscreet questions.
15. What does «boardwalk» mean?
16. I'll wake you up early.
17. There were thousands of birds on the trees.
18. He didn't want to have anything to do with them.
19. I don't understand his reason for leaving.
20. What happened between you and Maria?
21. Bob is right.
22. My mother has silverware for twenty people.
23. My sister is six years older than I am.
24. It seems like winter weather.
25. I don't like toast with jam.
26. Don't you think it's tiring to work with children?
27. There was thunder and lightning last night.
28. She is more intelligent than you think.
29. I want him to go to the store and buy milk.
30. He isn't very successful but he's happy.
31. The child is very sleepy.
32. He has a right to know what they do with his money.
33. Read it to me but not so fast.
34. I have some (a piece of/ Ø) good news for you.
35. I like it (him/her).
36. I tried liver yesterday and I liked it.
37. She wears very flashy jewelry.
38. Finish that, it's almost seven o'clock. I know. I'm coming.
39. The police received (a piece of/ Ø) information on the telex.

40. If you are hungry, there is food in the fridge.
41. If you are hot, open the window:
42. She has very long hair.
43. My father doesn't have gray hair.
44. Tomorrow you have to wake up very early to catch the bus.
45. When you have a fever, take an aspirin.
46. He is not married, but he has a mother-in-law.
47. He wants to be with her always.
48. I want to be a teacher when I grow up.
49. It's hot but I'm cold.
50. I think I've caught a cold.

Ejercicio 8

1. If you are not careful, you will break it.
2. I have a license but I don't have a car.
3. If you do it again, I'll spank you.
4. They make three million dollars a year.
5. Correct.
6. Correct.
7. He asked me a question I couldn't answer.
8. She doesn't want chocolate ice cream.
9. Correct.
10. He was green with envy.
11. She is not as old as I am.
12. If he weren't so jealous, she would love him more.
13. My father is a doctor and my brothers are doctors too.

14. I don't like eating with cheap silverware.
15. Never accept candy from a stranger.
16. I am afraid of not passing the exam.
17. Everyone is asleep but I don't feel sleepy.
18. Have you ever worked as a waiter?
19. He likes chicken but not turkey.
20. The party was so boring that everyone left early.
21. I don't know if I want you to do that.
22. Whenever it's windy, that window breaks.
23. Do you always have such bad weather in August?
24. Correct.
25. The man who died last week was very wealthy.
26. If he's right, we are in trouble.
27. He has had a fever for three days.
28. Correct.
29. I am really hungry.
30. He doesn't agree with my way of thinking.
31. I would like to get a new piece of (some new) furniture for the bedroom.
32. If you go to a boring movie, you are bored.
33. He didn't see his mother for ten years.
34. They are always arguing.
35. Men with gray hair are interesting.
36. That was a very important piece of (some important) information they gave us.
37. He has always had an interest in music.
38. Correct.
39. I am afraid when I walk down dark alleys alone.
40. No news is good news.

41. I don't know why he didn't do anything when they robbed his house.
42. You should spend a few days at my house in the mountains.
43. He was very successful (a big success) after his last movie.
44. John has never had a father.
45. I'll let you know when the dress is ready.
46. She has hair down to her waist.
47. Did you see E.T.? Yes, and I liked it.
48. I'm never hot.
49. Correct.
50. I don't have to put up with that nonsense.

Ejercicio 9

1. Whenever
2. boring
3. a car
4. dead
5. a fever
6. What's the matter with you?
7. information
8. is
9. than
10. early
11. the
12. anything
13. some good news

14. What does book mean?
15. I like it.
16. ask
17. some
18. His wife is very jealous.
19. an interest in
20. She wants an ice cream cone.
21. again
22. as a
23. bored
24. candy
25. be extra careful
26. I have a cold
27. a lawyer
28. for
29. a
30. didn't
31. ideal weather
32. two pieces of toast
33. tiring
34. is so successful
35. was asleep
36. is right
37. talking nonsense
38. not in my tea
39. two million dollars
40. ask
41. let
42. liver
43. I know

44. am in a hurry
45. short curly hair
46. a piece of furniture
47. anything
48. always
49. expensive equipment
50. do not agree

Verbos seguidos de diferente preposición en inglés y en español: ejercicios

Ejercicio 10

1. The mistake resulted in three deaths and several injuries.

2. The only thing he provided him with was affection.

3. He bought a radio that operates on batteries.

4. After having studied under the most renowned maestros in he world, he gave up the piano.

5. He lives by the work he does for his sister.

6. She laughed at all his jokes.

7. I have laughed at all his jokes.

7. I have known him for a long time and I trust him.

8. He is only nice to the people who might be able to help him.

9. I marvel (wonder) at his ability with a ball.

10. He hurt his leg in the accident.
11. The waitress was rude to all the customers.
12. David is married to the richest girl in town.
13. Those two events are not related to the crime.
14. He divorced her when he found out what she was doing.
15. The police were very polite to the demonstrators.
16. You don't have to pay for the ticket until you arrive.
17. He was fed up with his neighbors and he moved.
18. He taught his dog how to do many tricks.
19. She has never been engaged to anyone.
20. I'd like to learn how to play the piano.
21. Whether we go or not depends on the weather.
22. Do you know how to get home alone?
23. She delights in cold water.
24. He is named after the first president.
25. We decided on a small church in the old part of town.
26. He is capable of stealing candy from a small child.
27. You can't count on good weather.
28. I have been in love with you since the first moment I saw you.
29. I fell in love with my brother's girlfriend's sister.
30. The politician didn't want to comment on the defeat of his party.
31. Mary is next to the girl in pink.

32. He bet on a white horse in the fifth.

33. My house is near work.

34. He attended the dance only because she wanted him to.

35. The cheese was covered with green fungus.

36. He is mad (angry) at his sister because she didn't come.

37. He dreamed of being the best player on the team.

38. Gonzalo is not cruel to anyone.

39. She always dresses in black.

40. She is ill with tuberculosis.

41. He is indebted to all of his friends.

42. He filled the glass with water and drank it.

43. Vultures feed on the remains of other animals.

44. He concealed his private life from his fellow workers.

45. They supplied us with everything we needed to climb the mountain.

46. He always talks about things he doesn't understand.

47. I have just thought of a marvellous activity for the class.

48. You have to arrive at the airport two hours before the flight leaves.

49. He arrived in New York the day we were leaving.

50. I don't think the rise in the stock exchange is related to the elections.

Ejercicio 11

1. Correct.
2. Mark taught his daughters how to swim.
3. We are thinking of going to Italy this year.
4. Discriminating against people can be punished by law.
5. It's easy to be fed up with thirty-five-year-old children.
6. You only need to provide your children with food, shelter and affection.
7. The house was surrounded by trees.
8. His international acclaim resulted in his winning the Noble Prize.
9. The Pope approved of the cardinal's attitudes and actions concerning the conflict.
10. The President's plane arrived at the airport at six o'clock.
11. He paid for dinner and she bought the drinks afterwards.
12. The rise in prices is not related to the measures taken by the government.
13. It's easy to hurt people just by talking.
14. I am the worst at tennis in my class.
15. Be nice to your friends.
16. Correct.
17. Sometimes I wonder about his true intentions.
18. I don't attend the faculty meetings if I don't have to.
19. Correct.

20. The floor was covered with blood.
21. Nobody ever comments on his sordid past.
22. Phillip is mad at the whole family.
23. It's just as easy to fall in love with a rich girl.
24. I dreamed of (about) you last night.
25. I always bet on the underdog.
26. He pleaded with his boss to give him the day off.
27. A city's capability to organize the Olympics depends on public support of the idea.
28. If you are cruel to others, they are sure to be cruel to you.
29. You can't count on him to be there on time.
30. Correct.
31. She is very attractive when she is dressed in green.
32. Have you ever stolen anything from anyone?
33. Correct.
34. I don't trust him enough to leave him alone.
35. I don't like to go there because it reminds me of a bad experience.
36. Everyone laughed at her joke.
37. I've been ill with a cold for a month.
38. Arnold is married to Marvin's sister.
39. My boss congratulated me on a job well done.
40. There is a pharmacy near my house.
41. He was very rude to us when we came in.
42. Correct.
43. Deciding on the right school is not easy.
44. I was indebted to my parents after they helped me through college.
45. He is named after his father.

46. She was filled with excitement after winning the prize.
47. Mr. Sadin delighted in the pain of his guests.
48. Birds feed on worms and insects.
49. He doesn't know how to swim.
50. He hurt his head when he walked through the doorway.

Ejercicio 12

1. from
2. of
3. from
4. at
5. in
6. with
7. to
8. on
9. on
10. with
11. with
12. at
13. in
14. on
15. on
16. with
17. at
18. on
19. Ø
20. for

21. to
22. on
23. by
24. to
25. with
26. for
27. with
28. Ø
29. about
30. to
31. to
32. of
33. to
34. against
35. with
36. in
37. on
38. of
39. at
40. in
41. under
42. for-for
43. to
44. with
45. for
46. at-at
47. Ø
48. on
49. to
50. at

www.ingramcontent.com/pod-product-compliance
Lightning Source LLC
Chambersburg PA
CBHW052131270326
41930CB00012B/2837